THE VILLAGES OF GOA IN THE EARLY SIXTEENTH CENTURY

THE VILLAGES OF GOA IN THE EARLY SIXTEENTH CENTURY

POWELL, B. H. BADEN

GYAN

Published by

Gyan Publishing House
5, Ansari Road
Daryaganj, New Delhi-110002
Phone: 011-47034999, 9811692060
E-mail: books@gyanbooks.com

Distribution Network
gyanbooks.com
India, USA, Canada, UK, Australia

ISBN: 978-93-7447-175-3 (HB)

First Published, 1900

2nd Impression 2025

Printed at: Gyan Press, Delhi.

THE VILLAGES OF GOA IN THE EARLY SIXTEENTH CENTURY

Author: POWELL, B. H. BADEN

THE VILLAGES OF GOA

IN THE

EARLY SIXTEENTH CENTURY.

BY

B. H. BADEN-POWELL, C.I.E., M.R.A.S.

[*From the* "JOURNAL OF THE ROYAL ASIATIC SOCIETY," *April*, 1900.]

Art. XI.—*The Villages of Goa in the Early Sixteenth Century.* By B. H. Baden-Powell, C.I.E., M.R.A.S.

In the following pages I have endeavoured to present an account of the contents of a document, which needs some special acquaintance with the details of village history to understand it, but which possesses considerable interest since it is the earliest known account of a local group of Indian villages written by an European observer.

The document is an official charter or record of customs (*Foral dos usos e costumes*) dated September 16, 1526, under the authority of Don João, "King of Portugal, etc., and lord . . . . of the conquest, navigation, and commerce of Ethiopia, Arabia, Persia and India." The original (in Portuguese) forms No. 58 in Fasciculus 5 of the *Archivo Portuguez oriental.* This 'fasciculus' itself consists of three volumes, printed at Goa in 1863.

Mr. R. S. Whiteway has already published an abstract at p. 216 of his "Rise of the Portuguese Power in India, 1497–1550"[1]; but he has kindly placed at my disposal his manuscript translation of the original, and as there are several matters in it which deserve more specific record than his abstract gives, I have, with his help, reproduced the substance of the whole charter in somewhat greater detail. In so doing I have not followed the order of the clauses as they stand in the original; but have endeavoured to make the rules more intelligible, by bringing together under definite heads all that the charter contains on each subject. In the original, the various points are set down, apparently, as they occurred to the writer; so that often

[1] London, A. Constable, 1899. Mr. Whiteway (late of the Indian Civil Service) is also the author of the Settlement Report of the Mathura District, N.W.P., so valuable to students of Indian villages.

one or two clauses refer to a given subject, the writer passes on to another matter, and then more on the first subject is given in a later paragraph. At the same time, by always preserving the 'clause' number of the original, I have avoided any difficulty of reference.

It is needless, perhaps, to say, that the italics are my addition, because the matter is particularly noteworthy.

The abstract, so rearranged, is followed by a commentary: the capital letters in brackets added to the text, refer to the passages so marked in the commentary.

In the concluding pages I have endeavoured, with Mr. Whiteway's aid, to give some account of the history of these villages. This is very curious as showing how a village naturally constituted in one way, can undergo a complete transformation in the course of three centuries. And it is also instructive to note that the change was brought about by the effect of a radically bad system of revenue management, under which the responsibility for payment is enforced in a manner not adapted to the real village constitution. The headmen are allowed—indeed, are obliged—to make levies of rents and imposts over the village lands; and when they get into difficulties, they *sell the right to receive these dues*, in various fractions; thus they themselves lose their position and disappear, while the villages become dominated by a host of purchasers of 'shares' in the proceeds of the land—such sharers having no authority and no recognized position, but being naturally eager to make the most of their claims, are quite unscrupulous as to what they do in order to realize them.

Abstract of a Charter of 1526

(rearranged so as to bring together all the orders relating to the same subject).

Preamble.—The Roll (*Foral*) purports to be granted to the 'Gancars' or village headmen (**A**), cultivators, and taxpayers, dwellers in, and [permanent] residents of, the villages in the several islands that make up Goa.[1] The facts, i.e. the amount of revenue, "the rights [of possession], '*usos*' [subsidiary rights], and customs,"[2] are declared to have been recorded after inquiry, and by ascertaining what the people "paid to the kings and lords of the soil before it was ours." The figures of the Revenue Assessment were set down in a separate roll: the rights and customs are recorded in what follows.

I. *The Village Headmen, their origin and privileges.*

(Clause 1.) Every village has certain 'Gancars'; in some there are more, in others fewer, according to the custom of the village. The said word (Gancar) means governor, administrator, and benefactor, and was given because *in the old times there were four men to establish new cultivation in an island or other waste place.* These improved and cultivated the land so that in time there grew up a large inhabited site. And the founders, for their good government, administration, and work at the spread of cultivation, were called 'gancar' and became lords and superiors (*sogigadores*)[3] over the others, who agreed to pay rent and taxes so that they might remain possessed of their heritable rights and customs. *But the true origin of this is unknown* (A).

[1] It is hardly necessary to observe that the *Foral* refers, not to the whole of Goa as it now is (which contains in all 421 villages, many of them not in the condition here described), but only to that portion known as the 'Ilhas' or islands acquired sixteen years before the date of the charter. But in 1543 two other tracts, Salsette (Sāsti) and Bardes, were added, and the charter was made applicable to them also. Thus, the 31 villages to which the charter primarily refers, became only part of the area governed by the rules. From the legislation of 1882 we ascertain that at that time the 'Ilhas' contained 38 villages, Salsette 53, and Bardes 39. It may be remarked by the way, that the increase of 31 villages in 1526, to 38 in 1882, shows how very unprosperous must have been the condition of affairs, since only so small an increase of cultivation and population took place. The whole tract to which the charter refers is officially known as the 'Old Conquests' (*Velhas conquistas*).

[2] I think this is the meaning: the primary right is to a certain land holding, but to this there are subsidiary, customary rights of user, etc.

[3] = *subjugatores* or overlords, I apprehend.

(Clause 8.) In order to secure the position of the Gancars, because they are leaders and their office is hereditary, no Gancar (in his own village) can be removed from office—no matter what fault he may commit. Neither can the writer [Kulkarṇi], since he also holds an hereditary post and was appointed by the said headmen (*e foi posto pelos ditos Gancares*).[1] If either class commits a crime, there may be a penalty in person or goods; and if the punishment is death, the office passes on to the son or next heir. (Then follows a note of the authority that can try offences, according as they are of greater or less gravity.)

(Clause 17.) Should a Gancar *abscond* to avoid payment of his revenue, an assembly of the village called *Gancaria* (Gāṅwkaria) must be held, and a proclamation made for the fugitive. Should this be disregarded, his property will be taken over by the other Gancars [who are jointly liable with him], and they can transfer it to others. [I suppose this means they can farm it out.[2]]

(Clause 18.) But an absconding Gancar's heritable property [i.e. his *watan* or special holding as headman] cannot be taken from him. His heirs must be asked if they will take up the absconder's obligations: if they refuse, or if there are no heirs, *the other Gancars* take over the property, but not the moveable property which in the absence of [direct] heirs escheats to the Crown.[3]

(Clause 19.) If a Gancar or other person dies, or leaves

[1] This is repeated more than once in the charter. Originally in raiyatwāri villages generally, there can hardly be a doubt that the writer (mahato, pāṇḍyā, or kulkarṇi (Karn and Mar) = the Paṭwāri of Northern India) was introduced as part of the hereditary staff, as early as the time when the royal grain-share was first levied from all the cultivators. But in villages founded (as these evidently were) in the waste at a later date, it is quite possible that the writers may have been appointed by the leaders of the colonists.

[2] Mr. Whiteway tells me that in the *Archivo* there is a note stating that on the margin of the original *Foral* was found an (old) addition, to the effect that in one village ('Sancoale' of Salsette) it was the 'custom' to allow the nearest *Christian* heir to take the property (on paying arrears) in preference to others; and that failing such a convert, the natural heirs should take. In either case the absconder, if he returned, was allowed to recover his position.

[3] It will be seen, later, that the rules do not recognize *collateral*, but only direct, succession. Ordinarily 'the other' (recognized) Gancars in a village would be collaterals (brothers or cousins) of the absconder, not his sons.

the country, having no heirs, any revenue-free land escheats to the Crown [presumably, in view of Clause 18, other than *watan* land]. But debts of the deceased may be charged on it, provided a debt to the State ranks first for payment.

(Clause 40.) Should a Gancar of the Island of Chorão or others adjoining this island of Tissuary, fly from the country to the 'Moors' (Mussulmans), or in order to avoid paying his revenue, "as it is said they sometimes do, but we hope they will not do so in future," the moveable property will escheat [as already said], and the immoveable and the headmanship [i.e. the collective *watan*] will be sold *to the highest bidder who agrees to take up* the revenue-liability; and any surplus of the price realized, over and above arrears already due, will go to the Treasury. [By custom it was *only Gancars* who bid at such auctions: see clause 20, *post*. This clause (40) seems to repeat clauses 17, 18.]

II. *The Headmen's Precedence (among themselves).*

(Clauses 41, 42.) At a festival when piçhauris[1] and betel are distributed, the chief Gancar takes first, and the others in order of their grade; and in calling the roll of names, the order of precedence is to be observed.

(Clause 46.) At seed-time and at harvest, the first field to be taken in hand shall be that of the chief Gancar: and so with thatching the roofs with *olhas* (leaves of *Borassus* palm); the chief Gancar shall have his house thatched before the other houses.

(Clause 47.) The dancing girls shall go first and perform (*festejar*) before the house of the chief Gancar, and then before the others.

Gancars *of equal rank* are to receive betel, etc., standing side by side with their arms crossed so that the right hand of one may be below the left hand of the other: (then) if one says "I received it with my right hand," the other will

[1] I cannot find this (Hindi) word in the Marāthi dictionary; it means a small kerchief to cover the head, or scarf of honour.

be able to say, "My left hand was held above your right" [so that your right hand was not superior to mine].[1]

(Clause 48.) As to Gancars who are 'in community' [i.e. an undivided family], so that, at a ceremony, there is no pre-eminence of one or other, they may sell the honour of precedence for the occasion, to any Gancar in the village, at a price agreed on; and the price shall be distributed in the village: if no one purchases the honour, the writer [Kulkarṇi] may take it in their stead and so save a dispute.[2]

III. *The Status of the Villages.*

(Clause 2.) In the Goa territory there are 31 villages (a list is given); eight are placed at the head of the list, as "these are the chief for their privileges and pre-eminence" (**B**).

(Clauses 43, 44.) When a formal resolution regarding some matter is come to by all the villages assembled, and the decision is written down by the 'writer,' a formal reading and confirmation is called '*Nemo.*' This *nemo* is made by the chief headman present of the village Neura Kalān, because it is the chief village: in his absence the 'writer' makes it (**C**).

(Clause 45.) The village of Taleigão has this pre-eminence, that it *commences the rice harvest.* The headmen carry a bundle of rice to present it at the High Altar of the Cathedral. [This association of the village with the religion of the conquerors is very curious.] The Vicar of the Cathedral after this function accompanies the headmen to

[1] As no Oriental would receive with his left hand, the explanation is confusing. What is perhaps meant, is that, as the betel-giver is one person, he must necessarily approach one of the two right hands first, and so seem to give one a preference; whereas by arranging that one of the right hands is in a position of some inferiority, the difference is ceremonially neutralized.

[2] In Colonel Sykes' account of the Dakhan Villages, he relates a case where the whole of the various privileges attaching to a headmanship had to be partitioned; and it was arranged (by a pançāyat) that some of the honours or precedences should attach to one and some to the other sharers. In the above rule, if such a partition had not been made, and (say) three brothers were all Gancars by birth and so far equal, a solution of the difficulty is provided.

the Factory, and the Factor will spend 4 *pardaos*[1] in piçhauris, which he will put round the necks of the headmen: the other villages can then begin to cut their rice.

IV. *The Headmen's Duties in connection with the Revenue and the Cultivation.*

(Clause 3.) Each of the villages is bound to pay a certain rent (or revenue) as entered in a separate roll.

The headman assisted by the 'writer' *will distribute and assign the amount among the cultivators and those having lands,*[2] according to their customs and conditions of this charter. The headmen are bound to *distribute, collect, and pay the revenue or rent,* whether it increases or decreases, *and the loss or profit shall remain with them and with the village,* in order that the persons may bear the loss or share in the profit, who by custom (as before set forth) are entitled. Loss occasioned by war they shall be exempt from accounting for, according to the proportion of loss sustained by each holder.

(Clause 4.) The said profit and loss of each year shall be distributed, in proportion to each person's rent, on the palm or garden cultivation, or rice-land, which he holds (E).

(Clause 5.) Certain 'gardens' [bāghāit land of the modern Bombay system], palm-groves, and rice-lands are assessed to pay fixed sums,[3] so that even if there be loss, they do not contribute to make it up. Other lands (of these kinds), though they are assessed at certain rates, yet are obliged to contribute further towards losses when there are any.

[1] The coinage is described in Mr. Whiteway's "Rise of the Portuguese Power," p. 69. The *pardão* is valued at 360 *reals*, which at the time would have been worth rather more than 7*s*. 6*d*. If there were several headmen, perhaps as much as 30*s*. might be required to buy these scarves; but it is not probable that any very costly article was given.

[2] The distinction here, I think, is between the various holders of fixed or hereditary land and the cultivators of rice-lands (clause 20, *post*), who merely take the land at an auction for the year or harvest, or who otherwise have no hereditary holding.

[3] Apparently this is the udhaḍjamabandi, so common in the Bombay territories, where the holder is (for one reason or another) allowed to have a fixed lump sum assessed, which does not alter under any circumstances.

V. '*Watan*' *Grants for Village Service.*

(Clause 12.) Gancars can *give rent-free lands*, be they waste, or cultivated, but vacant, lands, *to the village servants*, i.e. the temple Brahman, the gate-keeper (*porteiro*), the '*rendeiro*,'[1] the washerman, cobbler, carpenter, blacksmith, temple-sweeper (*faraz* = farāsh), dancing girls, and the '*chocarreiro*.'[2] These persons *get rent-free holdings of garden or other land as the recompense of their services.* The grants are irrevocable, nor can any servant be removed and another man put in his place; for the servant is hereditary, and the grant is to him, his son, grandson, etc. Nor can servants be appointed other than the above-named, nor can they have free lands. Should such a grant lapse from failure of heirs, another man of the same profession must be put in to fill his place.

(Clause 13.) Headmen cannot, without express orders, make a rent-free grant to any person not a resident of the village.

VI. *Disposition of Village Lands that are vacant.*

(Clause 9.) Headmen can *grant land which is waste or fallow within the boundaries of their village* to any applicant who wishes to cultivate vegetables. ['garden' land] or

[1] *Rendeiro* in Portuguese may mean either one who receives, or one who pays, a rent or other charge or dues. I am unable to suggest definitely what person, regarded as one of the village staff, is meant. But it is quite possible that some 'bailiff' or other collector of the various imposts and levies was required (though not belonging to the original 'balute' staff), and so was put in and rewarded with a 'watan.' Such a person *is* alluded to in later documents as *saccador*, and it may be that the charter means the same thing by *rendeiro*.

[2] 'Chocarreiro' means a buffoon or jester—always implying jests of a low and coarse character. (So I am informed by an excellent Portuguese scholar at Lisbon.) I have never heard of any such person being one of the village staff. But the 'Mahār' (see J.R.A.S., April, 1897, p. 258) is constantly found; and in Marāthi (according to Molesworth) the Mahār is often alluded to as 'Chokhāmeḷā' (after the name of one of their tribal holy men). It seems to me possible that a Portuguese scribe hearing this word and not understanding it, may have put it down as 'Chocarreiro.' The Mahārs are always holders of *watan* land, and they are not otherwise mentioned in this list, though indispensable to the villages. There are generally several of them.

a grove, or for "other profitable use."[1] The grant is conditioned for the payment of such rent-rate as may seem fair [presumably a favourable or reduced rate] up to twenty-five years, after which the full customary rate will be payable. The customary rate is for each plot (grove) of twelve paces broad, that is, from palm-tree to palm-tree, up to one hundred trees; for the whole of it, five '*tanga*' of four '*barganim*' to the *tanga* (F). At this rate they pay for the extent, greater or less, of land held. The headmen may grant waste land to make a grove or garden for less than the rate of five *tanga*, but not for more; and may issue a written grant.

(Clause 10.) Land granted to make a betel-garden[2] will be given at the following rates:—5 cubits × 5 cubits (which is from one betel-vine to another) up to 100 plants: if irrigated by well, 4 *barganim* [i.e. 1 *tanga*] annually; if irrigated by running stream, 6 *barganim* [i.e. 1½ *tanga*] (F).

Once granted, all such lands become hereditary possessions: this is the general rule, but if there is in any village some special custom in the matter, it will be given effect to.

(Clause 20.) The rice-lands[3] of each village, according to the custom, will be put up to auction and knocked down to the highest bidder; this *does not apply to such lands when they are private property as heritable lands*. The bidding is to be among residents of the village, unless any special custom allows non-residents to bid.

[Bidding was, by custom, for many years, confined to headmen.]

[1] Apparently wet land (suited for rice) is not included, as that is disposed of in another way (clause 20, *post*). Apparently also the 'dry' crop of the Dakhan (jirāit) is not known in the Goa climate; rice, vegetables, etc., palm-groves, and betel-gardens are the staple.

[2] These gardens for the aromatic leaf (betel) (*Piper betle*), used with areca-nut for chewing, can only be made in favourable soil and with careful irrigation. They are very profitable. The (climbing) plants are often protected overhead with mats.

[3] Low-lying and flooded lands only suited for rice, which is here the chief crop.

VII. *Failure of a whole Village.*

(Clause 6.) Should any village be so destroyed that it can no longer pay us the revenue assessed on it, the Gancars shall notify the 'Chief Thānadār' and the 'writer of the Island,' who will inquire into the causes of the failure; if they find it to be true, *they will call the headmen of the eight principal villages.* Other headmen may be present, but, by custom, the affairs of the Island lie with the headmen of the eight. To such an assembly, the headmen of the disabled village may relinquish the management. The eight must accept the charge as they are bound, and will put the village up to auction (in presence of the officials mentioned) and make it over to the highest bidder.

The deficiency [difference between the sum bid and the normal revenue] is to be made good by distributing the amount *over the eight* villages, *or over the whole* island, viz. on those properties which are liable to make good losses, in such way that the full amount of our revenue shall in any case be made good to us.[1]

The lessee or lessees of the village are bound to improve and restore the disabled lands during the term of their lease, and for this purpose they shall hold the office of Gancar.

(Clause 7.) But the regular hereditary Gancars are not by this means permanently ousted; they must be restored whenever they ask for restitution and offer to pay the revenue-demand. When the lease has expired, the lessees have no further claim (**D**).

VIII. *Rules of Inheritance.*

(Clause 30.) The order of succession is from father to son and grandson, etc., and [failing the direct descending

[1] Nothing is said as to *when* 'the eight' and when the whole body of cultivators in the island (not holding free, or at any fixed rates) can be called on. Probably the headmen will decide, according to which gives the best prospect of making up the deficit.

line] upwards to father, grandfather, etc. No female can inherit.

(Clause 27.) If a man [however] has no sons, etc., *his property will escheat to the Crown, and not go in the ascending line even if his father is alive*; unless, indeed, the deceased was holding undivided with his father.[1]

Among sons the division is equal; if partition takes place in the father's lifetime, the father is entitled to maintenance.

If one son dies without heirs, his share lapses to the Crown, unless it is an undivided share, when it falls to the surviving co-sharers. A share of revenue-free land in any case lapses to the Crown (cf. clause 19). Should one of the brothers turn Mussulman or abandon the world and become a jogi, "which is the same as the gipsies (*ciganos*)" in Portugal (!), the property lapses to the Crown; but, *if it is revenue-paying land*, it will be sold and the private debts first discharged.[2]

(Clauses 28, 29.) Need not be detailed; they contain the rule that where property will escheat to the Crown, the dead man cannot be buried or cremated (as the case may be) before the officials have notice, and that they may take account of the estate. The property is put up to sale by auction to the Gancars and relatives only. Some preference is given to the relatives (who consent to discharge the revenue liability). Clause 29 relates to moveable property (**D**).

(Clause 32.) The principle of division when there are sons by two wives is, to divide *per stirpes* [= jorubānṭ in N.W. India, or çūnḍavanḍ in the Panjāb] and not *per capita*; [so that four sons of one wife would get one-half between them, and one son of the other wife the whole of the other share. This, Mr. Whiteway notes, was modified by a later order allowing either rule according to custom as established.]

[1] No notice is taken of the ordinary rule, that failing the downward or upward direct line, the collaterals come in, brothers and brothers' sons. These are thus disinherited by the rules, which claim everything for the Crown.

[2] See also clause 19 (which includes "other persons" as well as Gancars) regarding revenue-free land.

IX. *Rules about Alienation of Land.*

(Clause 15.) Should a Gancar *or other person* desire to sell *any heritable property* in the village, he must obtain the consent of all the Gancars of the village in question. And no one can purchase without similar permission.

Any bargain made without such consent is *ipso facto* voidable, and can be set aside if the Gancars so desire in the interest of the revenue collection for which they are responsible. A purchaser is to receive a written slip, noting the revenue on the land bought, to save mistakes and discontent.

(Clause 16.) It is not sufficient that the sellers of heritable property sign the deed of sale: all his heirs must sign also; and if one of them is a minor, there must be a consent signed by his guardian or next friend on his behalf.

Omission of any necessary signature renders the transaction voidable at any time; but if a transaction is set aside, the purchase-money must be returned, though the purchaser will have no claim to be compensated for improvements he may already have effected.

X. *Rules of Procedure.*

(Clause 11.) The writer of the 'Camara' (Chamber or State Council ?) of the Island, must be present at the passing and establishing, called '*Nemo*,' of all agreements and resolutions such as are issued by the Chief Gancars of all the island together with the Chief Thānadār and writer, etc. Without the writer of the Island nothing can be done; for he takes note and assents to all, so that he may decide any doubts or question that may afterwards arise. In like manner [in a village matter] the village writer must be present. The writer's records (village books) regulate all the villages in the islands.[1] I may

[1] "The islands" of old Goa territory are here (and elsewhere) mentioned as Tissuary, Diwary, Chorão, and Jua. (See note to the Preamble.)

add to this that, by orders issued in 1735, the 'writer' (*Escrivão*) was directed to enter the 'nemos' in consecutively paged books, under penalty of being whipped and banished for five years to Timor (equivalent to a sentence of death). The editor notes on this that the 'nemos' are often found recorded on loose sheets; the order defeated itself by its severity.

(Clause 14.) When the chief officers summon a general meeting of Gancars in the Island, all must attend or at least get a local meeting to choose a deputy to appear in their stead. At such a local meeting (*Gancaria*) every Gancar must attend, or at least an heir of an absent member. The "usual penalty" will be exacted from anyone intentionally absent.

(Clauses 22–26.) Are of less interest, having no direct relation to village constitution. They lay down rules of evidence: e.g., claims to immoveable property must be supported by written evidence, confession of judgment, or by village records. If the latter are lost, there may be a solemn oath taken in the Temple of 'Uzoo.'[1]

Money loans are next regulated. A larger sum than 50 *tangas* must not be lent except on a written bond. If otherwise, the parties may agree to refer the matter to "two selected men" for decision.

Interest is allowed at one *barganim* for every six *tangas*. [One in 24, or a little over 4 per cent., if it is *per annum*; but more probably it is *per mensem*, in which case it is nearly 50 per cent.] (F.)

But interest can never be more than double the principal. [The other clause excludes, as do the Hindu law books, certain persons from giving evidence; among them children under 16, 'gardeners,' day-labourers, sons of a prostitute, variously defective persons: these, though incompetent in serious cases, may testify in minor ones.]

[1] What this means, I cannot ascertain. Mr. Whiteway has also been unable to interpret it.

XI. *Miscellaneous.*

(Clause 21.) The village headmen are liable to provide (unpaid) labour (begāri) from any dwellers (*pelos moradores*) in the village, to clear away bushes and weeds from the city walls and '*cavas*' (ditches?), also "to meet other necessities as occasion may arise."

(Clauses 37, 38, 39.) The village must feed the Chief Thānadār and his clerks, when visiting the place officially. Also "our factor" and his officials. Every 'peon' sent on official message is to be allowed (during his stay) two measures of rice daily and one *real* to buy bẹtel.

(Clause 34.) Officials must not take bribes, nor accept lands, nor trade within their jurisdiction, etc.

(Clause 35.) Should the Gancar make any demands on the village for "clothes or sweetmeats, or other benefits" for himself or for any official or person, each Gancar will be liable to pay a sum equal to the whole demand from all the villages, and this sum by way of fine shall be given one half to the informer and the other half for the benefit of 'prisoners' (*e a outra para os captivos*).[1] A village writer, if in the conspiracy to make the levy, shares in the penalty.

(Clause 32.) Claims all treasure-trove for the Crown. (The Hindu law claims *half*) (**D**).

(Clause 31.) Disposal of a man, who is a thief, caught with the stolen property in his possession, if he "have an owner" (i.e. is a slave), he is made over to his master—by way of concession, "though by use and custom he belongs to us."

(Clause 49.) Use of the torch, palankeen, or umbrella, is a privilege requiring license of the Governor, unless it is an hereditary honour. When granted as an honour, the grant may either leave the grantee to employ his own

[1] Mr. Whiteway kindly informs me that this means either the half is to go towards the fund for redeeming captives in the hands of 'the Moors' (a frequent provision), or else to help support the Goa prisoners, who depended on charity. The former is more probable, and the clause was perhaps slipped in at Lisbon, as an improvement on the original.

servants and buy his own oil (for the torch), or may grant the oil and servants at cost of the State. Each emblem may be granted by itself—or all together—in either way.

Commentary.

General Observations. — The villages, throughout the Bombay country and the Dakhan, and Konkan generally, are in the raiyatwāri or 'severalty' form, marked by distinctive (and ancient) features, viz.: (i) The allotment of a separate (heritable) holding to every cultivating family (i.e. there is nothing in the nature of a unit estate or property shared in fractional proportions among a body of the same descent). (ii) It is marked by the existence of certain privileged holdings (*watan*) which are the reward of village service, or are also the special heritable property (along with rights of precedence) of the village officers in virtue of their position. (iii) By the influence and power of the headman (and his family). Such an officer has a real indigenous title in the local languages,[1] and is quite unlike the modern and purely official representative called 'lambardār' in N.W. India.

I make this observation because it is clear from every part of the *Foral* of 1526 that the villages (of the old Goa territory) therein described were *then* in the same form, and that every mark or feature of this constitution is mentioned. We shall afterwards see that the villages have since undergone a complete change.

As regards the Dakhan villages, I have already fully discussed[2] the changes which were introduced by the dominating position (at an early but uncertain date) of

[1] The Marāthi is Pātīl; Gāṅwkār (Karn). In other countries where the raiyatwāri form is indigenous, there are also many local names—Maṇḍal, Mānki, Gauḍā, etc., etc. In the northern form of joint-village no headman—properly so-called—exists, and there is no *indigenous* name or word. The (official) headman recognized by the administration is known either by the Arabic word muqaddam, introduced by the Moslem revenue officers, or by our (half-English) word lambar-dār (number-holder).

[2] J.R.A.S., April, 1897, p. 241 foll.

superior families, the memory of whose possession was long preserved in the name 'mirāsi' land, which continued to attach to certain parts of the villages and which indicated a certain privileged tenure, and survived long after the old 'overlord,' co-sharing, families had disappeared. No change of this kind appears in the present case; no such special lands existed, as far as any indications in the *Foral* are concerned. Indeed, I doubt whether this Dakhan peculiarity, and the distinction of 'mirāsdār' and 'upri' (common cultivator) extended so far south as (e.g.) the district of Belgām, which adjoins Goa. The distinction in the Goa villages was rather (at least in later times) between the mere contract-tenants put in by the managers, or auction-purchasers of the cultivating right in the rice lands for one harvest, and the permanent holders of heritable lands (kuḷāçāri)—a term which included both rent-payers and those who had rent-free lands ('watan,' etc.). (Kuḷā = a family paying revenue to Government.)

It was, I think, the conditions under which this group of villages grew up, as well as the Moslem system of revenue—the worst features of which the rules preserve—that prepared the way for the change which in later times came over these villages.[1] I do not mean to suggest that we possess any detailed information of the earliest or pre-Mughal Moslem system. But the system described in the *Foral* certainly differed widely from that of the older Hindu

[1] It will be remembered that the Goa territory in question had been under 'Hindu' (Kadamba) kings of Banavāsi, up to A.D. 1312. Then for some 60 years it was under early Moslem rule; after that, Hindu rule (but under Vijayanagar) was restored till A.D. 1449; when Moslem supremacy, first under the united Dakhan kingdom, and then under the separate Bijāpur ('Ādil Shāhi) dynasty, was once more established. There is nothing to indicate that the villages of the 'Ilhas' are very ancient; rather they seem to have been the result of a colonizing enterprise, headed by a few energetic men who founded the first villages. And we can fairly form some general idea of time which elapsed from the founding up to A.D. 1526, by allowing time for the increase of the first four or eight villages to the then existing number of 31. Nevertheless, the *form of the village*, as exhibited in the rules, is very much the same as that of the oldest 'raiyatwāri' villages in Central and Western India that are traceable. The headman, the privileged holdings, and the revenue paid to the king, are features mentioned in inscriptions and literary references of unquestionably ancient date.

kings, and in principle represents the Moslem plan. From all we know of the 'Hindu' kingdoms and overlordships (whether of Dravidian or of partly Aryan connection) it is certain that the royal revenue was derived from a share (in kind) of the grain produce of every holding or allotment (except certain privileged ones). The share (as such) was fixed by custom, and was not increased till comparatively late times, when rulers assumed the right to take such proportion as they appointed; and even then they sometimes tried to conceal the fact.[1] In any case it depended on the harvest; it was a share of what was actually produced and no more. But the Muhammadan system (of the Dakhan Kings) had been in force about seventy-five years, of which the last ten or twelve before the Portuguese conquest represented the more defined and stricter system of the 'Ādil Shāhi kings. This system, besides assessing the revenue-demand in money, created a *liability for a total sum from each village*, which before was unknown; and it accordingly must have given the headman so extensive a power of arranging this and that holding—leasing this and charging that—that in time, although the system never permitted the headmen actually to buy up or appropriate the holdings in their own right, every plot of land (except a few favoured with freehold or fixed rates) must have been so charged with levies and imposts, that its possession was more a burden than a profit.

(A) The Portuguese form 'Gancar' in the text unquestionably refers to a governing and managing headman. It is true the Marāthi word, which is Gāṅwkar (or Gāṅwkari) means 'villager' in general; and Gooddine's Report (1852) mentions that *in the Dakhan* the term was applied to distinguish the (superior) holders of 'mirāsi' land *as well* as

[1] As (e.g.) when the Vijayanagar minister insisted on having the share paid in husked rice instead of 'paddy,' which of course largely increased the real payment without ostensibly altering the share.

the village headman; they were collectively denominated '*the* Gāṅwkar' or 'people of the village' *par excellence*.[1] But Molesworth notes that from about where 'Malwan' is marked on the map, the word becomes *used for the headmen only*. This change is, I believe, explained by the fact that the area of the Konkani-Marāthi language here merges into the territory where Kanarese is spoken, and in the latter Gāṅwkār (with the long *ā*) always means 'headman,' not 'villager.' It is *this* form that is represented by the Portuguese 'Gancar,' 'Gancares' (pl.).

The *Foral* of 1526 describes the 'headman' in all his original prominence, and with new powers. The word 'Gancar' does not (of course) etymologically mean 'Governor' or anything of the kind; but practically that is what the headmen's function became, the 'Subjugator' of the village.

The account given in clause 1 is confessedly tentative; but there may have been some genuine old tradition that "four men"—four brothers or associates—started the original colonization of the four islands (Tiswāḍi, Diwāḍi, Chorāo, and Jūa). If so, it is quite possible that eight villages, which we may suppose to have been the first fully equipped and separately constituted groups, had the pre-eminence (clause 2).[2]

The headman's position, it will be observed, is made up of his special holding of *watan* land, his (mānpān or) dignity and precedence, and his authority in the village. The whole together constitute, in fact, the *watan*. This is hereditary, and therefore becomes the property of the joint-family in the next succession. And the sons are all (at least called) Gāṅwkār (or Pātīl as the language may require). In the Dakhan we sometimes hear of each member of the family

[1] J.R.A.S., April, 1897, p. 268.

[2] It is curious to remark in the *Imperial Gazetteer* (in the note on Goa compiled from Dr. J. N. da Fonseca's account) it is mentioned that when Albuquerque made his entry into Goa after the conquest (March 1st, 1510) "eight leading men" presented him with the keys. But all the early historians agree that these eight were Muhammadans, so that it could not refer to the 'Gancares.'

taking the duty of office for a period, in rotation. In other cases, where the area was sufficiently large, the sons might get the village made into sections, resulting in separate villages distinguished as 'Khurd' and 'Kalān' (or 'Budrukh'). This process was known as a 'tarfbandi' under the Moslems.[1]

In the *Foral* (clause 2) we are told that the number of 'Gancares,' greater or less, was a matter of custom. That is to say, that though the Gancar family all had their share in the 'watan,' it would not follow that all would exercise the official functions of 'headman.' We are left, however, to conjecture whether the villages were divided into definite sections with one man (belonging to the family) over each; and whether that person was selected, as the eldest son of each principal branch from the ancestral founder, or how. It is evident (from the later papers) that the 'Gancares' did become very numerous,[2] but there must have been some rule as to the limited number required to perform public duty and make the allotment of lands, etc. Probably the number existing at the time of the *Foral* which was known, but is not stated, was adhered to, in this respect.

The village writer (Kulkarṇi) is also alluded to as one of the village superiors. Here it is (more than once) said that he was originally appointed by the headmen, though the office once given became hereditary (and *watandār* like others). In a case like this it is quite probable that the 'writers' were called in (with or without the local ruler's sanction) by the colonizers or founders of the villages, who would (under Hindu rule at any rate) enjoy considerable exemptions from taxation and much freedom. Ordinarily, we believe the 'writer' to have been introduced, rather by the king or his local officers, to look after his revenue collections.

(B) Not only do we observe that eight villages are superior in rank, but two among the eight have some extra

[1] Cf. J.R.A.S., April, 1897, p. 254.

[2] Goa never knew Mahrātha rule, as the Dakhan did; had it done so, these headmen would probably have been repressed and not allowed to act in the way we shall afterwards see they did.

dignity. The whole of the facts stated point to a strong probability, that we have here a case in which the traditional "four men," or other small number of leaders, went forth with a party of colonists and set on foot an area of cultivation, which at first began with two, and soon resolved itself into eight, villages, of which the leaders and their sons were the Gāṅkwārs. As time went on, fresh patches of cultivation, with their hamlets for residence, sprang up all round, and these in time attracted their own staff of artizans, and acquired a separate existence and place in the records. Thus (in the district originally comprised in the rules of 1526) there were 31 villages, all sprung, by extension and fission, from an original parent, or rather, a small number of parents.[1]

(C) I am not sure what this ceremonial reading out and writing down, of a general order or decision is. The Portuguese word *nemo* can hardly have anything to do with the Persian 'nāma'; I think it must refer to the Marāthi phrase 'nem (or niyam) lāoṇeṅ,' which means 'finally to confirm,' 'set up' or 'establish' anything.

(D) The various rules under the head of 'management' show how much the system has advanced in favour of the State Treasury; particularly the rule in the case of failure of a whole village strikes us as very harsh; for here the other villages, not the treasury, are to bear the loss, although they are in no wise to blame for it.[2] Moreover, the rules of 'escheat' (on failure of heirs) have been largely extended to benefit the Government, and collateral succession is not recognized. Nothing of the kind was known to ancient custom.

(E) The reader will probably fail to understand what can be meant by 'profit and loss' in the yearly revenue management. Ordinarily, where the revenue is assessed on

[1] We are quite familiar with this process in Northern India, where the parent site is called kheṛa, etc., and the offshoot villages, majrā, garhi, etc. See my "Indian Village Community" (Longmans, 1896), p. 276 foll.

[2] It is possible, however, that 'custom' may to some extent have justified the rule, if the villages, having developed out of an original central location, still regarded themselves as (in some sense) all one great village.

the whole village and properly distributed among the co-sharers (according to their constitution), as in North-Western India, the only question is of profit or loss to the cultivator or owner. And so in a Bombay raiyatwāri village, every holding bears its own assessment. The State Revenue *can* be no more than the *sum* of these assessments; and there is no question of profit or loss except to the cultivator himself—if the produce is so poor that it does not do more than barely meet expenses, and pay the revenue.

But under the method recorded as 'customary' by the *Foral*, the total amount which the 'Gancars' realize by the proper dues assessed on the several classes of heritable land may not equal the total sum for which they are made responsible by clause 4. In that case (saving only as regards loss due to war) the difference between the realized amount and the required total has to be made good by a surcharge, or further contribution demanded for such lands as are not expressly exempt. This may not, at once, be clear.

It appears from the rules that the village lands include (1) *Watan* lands of the headmen, writer, and village servants; these do not pay any rent or revenue. (2) There may be also other lands granted rent-free. (3) Also lands at a fixed assessment which does not vary, and there is no liability to any cess or surcharge. (4) There may be newly established fields, and vacant lands taken up (as arranged by the headman, clause 9), which, on the lease terms being accepted, become regular holdings. These are all 'heritable lands,' and are in effect private property. We gather from later documents that these holders of land at fixed rates, or on any permanent tenure, were called 'culacharin,' i.e. kuḷāçāri (Mar.), meaning 'rent-payers'—those who have a fixed *status* (cf. Wilson, Gloss., s.v. *kuḷā*). (5) But a large area of low-lying and flooded rice-land is included in each village (apart from any lands of this class that happen to be private property), and this does not become the property of anyone in particular, but is put up in convenient lots to auction every year, so that the rents bid may be devoted to meeting the State Revenue-demand in the first instance. In fact, the sum thus realized is probably the sheet anchor. If prices are high and circumstances favourable, the rice-lands may fetch such a sum that, together with the rents due on other lands, the total may more than cover the State demand, and there is a 'profit' which is distributed by a return payment to the persons entitled. Sometimes it will be the case that the total obtained will not cover the State demand; then the holders of lands that are not revenue-free, or on absolutely fixed terms, must make up the loss *pro rata*. It will be observed that the total State revenue is not 'permanently' assessed; it may increase or decrease whether by the effect of a periodical reassessment, or revision of settlement, or otherwise.

Under the later Moslem Settlements in the Dakhan, this system was not pursued: there, the headmen were equally made responsible for a total sum, but when they could not get enough out of the village to make it up, they did not formally redistribute the deficit as these rules direct, but had to pay it themselves, and were allowed to collect an annual 'mushāhara' or cash allowance, which (on the average) recouped them. It is hardly necessary to add that (under either system) great power is put into the hands of the headmen.

(F) Clause 9 is interesting as showing that the *tanga* = ṭaṅkā (Mar.) was a coin then in use. There is considerable confusion about the date, and the value, of the coins so called: the more so as '*tanga*' is still used in Goa, but for a copper coin = $\frac{1}{12}$ of the Goa rupee. In the latter case the word seems to be confused with 'ṭakā,' used for copper coin generally. It is said by Grant Duff that the silver 'ṭaṅkā' was introduced in 1637 into the Dakhan, and into the Nizām Shāhi kingdom some twenty-seven years earlier.[1] Here, however, we have a silver coin of this name in 1526. The ṭaṅkā is variously given as either four or nine 'māsha' of silver (1 māsha = 13 to 17 grains). It

[1] Quoted, J.R.A.S., April, 1897, p. 269.

is, however, clear that in the times of the *Foral*, the 'tanga' was a silver coin worth 60 *reals* or *reis*, and (at the then price of copper) was in value about sixteen pence. It consisted of four '*barganim*,' which appears to be the (Hindi) bārakāṇi. The old mediaeval ṭankā of the Pathān Empire was divided into fractions (kāṇi), of which one was $= \frac{1}{64}$. And there were various small coins, one of which was the 'duāzdah-kāni' (or bāra-kāni), i.e. twelve sixty-fourths. This would be nearly $\frac{1}{4}$ of the ṭankā, or about 4*d.* in value. (See Yule & Burnell, Supplement to Glossary, s.v. *bargani*; and Mr. Whiteway's "Rise of the Portuguese Power, etc.," p. 69.)

Later History of the Villages.

There are a number of later documents, and some legislative enactments, which show, as I have already indicated, that these (originally raiyatwāri) villages have since undergone a great change. Obscure as are the details of the change, there can be no doubt as to its occurrence, or as to its general nature.

It will help to make the matter more intelligible if I call to mind the fact that in India we are quite familiar with historic alterations in the constitution of villages.

Take for example the (very common) origin of 'pattidāri,' i.e. ancestrally-shared, villages in the North-West Provinces. They arose out of a *transformation of an earlier community*. There was once such a community—no matter how constituted—but enjoying a certain independence. But in the early days of British rule, when the idea of *one landlord* for each village or other estate was still prevalent, a revenue-farmer, or land-manager, got himself recognized, and was recorded, as *the* proprietor of the whole. In the course of some generations, his sons, grandsons, and great-grandsons, succeeding to the inheritance, made the village into shares; they became the founders of the 'patti,' 'thok,' and 'ṭūla' divisions. Within these, the co-sharers gradually multiplied, set up their managing 'pañçāyat,' and became *the* community

—the original body having sunk to being 'tenants,' and *their* constitution (whatever it was) having long disappeared.[1]

Or take another case — of the reverse process. In the Thāṅsra Tāluka of the Kaira district (North Bombay), about the year A.D. 1483, the Sultan *granted* ninety square miles of land to a number of his soldiers who had distinguished themselves at the storming of a noted fort not far off. A certain number of 'village' groups were taken possession of, or newly established, in this area. At first, if we may judge from the name 'Bāragām,' they were about twelve in number. These threw off hamlets in the usual way, and thus new villages developed. In all there were (in 1872) about twenty-seven. Originally they were held free of revenue; but the Mahrāthas had subjected them to a full assessment, and so they continued. These villages were in fact (though it was not the Bombay custom so to recognize them) 'pattidāri' villages, the descendants of the military grantees being the co-sharing owners (in fractional shares). At the Survey Settlement it was actually proposed to the communities that they should be (jointly) assessed at a lump sum for each village, they dividing the responsibility according to their own ancestral shares or constitutional method. But by that time the 'Maliks' (so they were called owing to the ownership originally granted them) had become so numerous, and the divided shares so small and in such poverty, that they feared the joint-responsibility and declined it.[2] The Government officers then dealt wisely with the case; they allowed each 'house' to hold its 'gharkheḍ' or private family land (what we should call 'sīr' in North-West India) revenue-free, and separately assessed and surveyed the other lands, making them 'raiyatwāri,'

[1] This, as a well-known fact, is the origin of a not inconsiderable number of villages (of this particular class) in the N.W.P.

[2] This shows how much revenue management depends on the character and customs of the people; liabilities cannot be created by administrative measures. And doubtless in Bombay the general prevalence of the *raiyatwāri* management served as an example to these villages, making them desire it. The poverty had been largely promoted by the exactions of the Mahrātha rulers and the Chief of Bālāsinūr; but was also due to excessive subdivision of the land among the families.

each holder having to pay the revenue direct to the local treasury. The only distinction was that (in virtue of their original superior position) the old proprietary families were granted a cash allowance (at a rate approximating to fifty per cent. on the assessment). Thus the 'Māliki' tenure (as a special one) has disappeared; the villages became ordinary raiyatwāri villages, only that certain families have a privilege in revenue-free (inām) lands, and a rentcharge or allowance (paid through the treasury) on the other (raiyat) holdings. I mention this case in some detail because in principle it represents *just what ought to be done with the old Goa villages.*

In the transformation which the villages of the *Foral* underwent, we have a greater complication. In the cases just stated the change is entirely intelligible because it directly refers to the shares or holdings in land, and to the consequent joint or separate liability for revenue. But in the Goa case, the land holdings, as such, were not affected. It was the rents and proceeds of land, not the land itself, that became the subject of the confused rights which appear at the present day.

The root of the mischief was (and perhaps still is) over assessment of the revenue, and the exaction of other dues besides. And this was aggravated by the fact that the whole revenue charge was made into one lump sum, and the headmen (according to their recognized number) were made jointly responsible to produce it somehow. It is true that the *Foral* declares this to be "the custom." But it was certainly not the old custom of the village; it was the (arbitrary) 'custom' of the Bijāpur Kings.

Nor can it for one moment be supposed that the revenue-demand was merely the aggregate of the properly adjusted, several assessments and lease-rents, duly allowing for rent and revenue-free lands, *watan* lands, and privileged holdings. It was a round sum arbitrarily made up, not of course entirely without reference to *data*, but in excess of any such total, because of the area of rice-land and other unappropriated holdings and waste land, which the headmen were expected to bring under cultivation, if they were expert and diligent.

But in truth the revenue-demand was almost certainly liable to arbitrary increase by the harsh rules of 'escheat' and the limitation of rights of inheritance, which would cause lands bearing additional revenue to be put on the list from time to time. And we find that in 1541, the revenue- (and rent-)free grants of even the village servants were withdrawn! Moreover, from certain rules in 1735 we learn that the ecclesiastics had been in the habit of demanding tolls from the village under the name of 'alms' (*esmolas*), and of imprisoning the villagers and distraining their goods to get payment. By the orders in question this custom was prohibited, but they show that it had long existed.

Under ordinary circumstances the extensive power thus put in the hands of the headmen would have made them *de facto* owners of all the village land, or at least have made all the holders (that were not rent-free) their subservient tenants. And this would have been followed by the headmen (as revenue-farmers) dividing the revenue-liability into definite (fractional) shares, and the village lands into corresponding shares. But it does not appear that any such stage actually developed. It is indeed necessary to suppose that the Gancars had *some* method of apportioning the revenue-responsibility among themselves—either by taking fractional shares of the money total, or by allotting the area and each headman becoming responsible for the proportion of revenue that fell on his particular portion. Curiously, no mention is made of anything of this kind. Nevertheless it is certain that the Gancars had no power to sell the village lands, whether in the hands of 'culacharins' (p. 281) or otherwise. They devoted themselves, therefore, to getting the largest total proceeds from rents of leased lands, auction-rents of rice-lands, dues and levies from hereditary landholders, etc., etc. That such landholders remained in existence is certain, since 'culacharins' are mentioned in the latest papers.

As long as matters went tolerably well, these total proceeds (supplemented by others to be mentioned presently) would make a sum somewhat larger than the revenue-demand: at least there was always the hope that it would do so, or could be made by good management to do so. Consequently the headmen, either with a view of saving themselves trouble, or being under the necessity of raising money on the security of the future collections, began to *sell shares* in the prospective proceeds of the village to persons who were neither headmen, nor village residents, nor landholders. In one village, it is noted that one person bought up the whole of the income; in another, there were some hundreds of purchasers of shares in the proceeds, contending with as many Gancars.

In 1604 some ineffectual efforts were made to prevent such sales.

The purchasers of shares in the proceeds of land taxation were called 'cuntocar' = (I suppose) to khūṅṭakār (Mar.). In Hindi, 'khūnt' means a share in land; but in Konkan-Marāthi 'khūṅṭa' means a 'peg'—hence a lot or share marked out or defined for purposes of taxation.

It is almost impossible to explain further how these 'shares' arose or on what they are based. The Portuguese authorities give no clue: they speak of them as 'tanga shares,' or as we might say 'rupee shares.'[1] In Northern India nothing is commoner than to find a whole village treated as 'one bīghā' or 'one rupee,' and then the shares are expressed in the customary subdivisions in the scale of land-measure or of money as the case may be. Thus we have a 'biswa' share, or a 'four-ana' share, meaning in the one case $\frac{1}{20}$ and in the other $\frac{1}{4}$, and so on. This arose when people had no idea of the 'vulgar fractions' of our arithmetic.

But in Goa the 'shares' are certainly *not fractions of land or rights in land*: they appear, as I said, to be fractions of

[1] Mr. Whiteway refers to the "Oriente Conquistado," vol. i, 171; but the suggested explanation there offered is quite meaningless. Other writers frankly confess their ignorance.

the estimated or prospective income derivable either from certain specified divisions or plots or allotted claims (khūṅṭa) of the village, or of the income derived from several different *heads of collection.*[1] Perhaps it is both. We know that in the Dakhan villages (under the Moslem system) there were two main heads of collections—(i) the various rents and cesses taken from the cultivated land-holdings (kālī), and (ii) those taken from the village-site in connection with houses, shops, village trade, and export, etc. (pāṇḍhri). If something of the kind became customary in the Goa villages, it would be quite natural. And it is not difficult to imagine that the income from each main division might be again classified under various sub-heads and separately dealt with. The land-income would be that from the fixed rents of the kuḷāçāri, from the auctioned rice-lands, from the vacant holdings, from the leased lands, and (very likely) from several imposts on the free lands. Thus the income under each head might be 'farmed' in (few or many) portions to as many 'sharers.' I only suggest this as possible under the circumstances of the case. Whatever, then, the nature of the 'cuntocar' or sharer's interest, there must soon have been an *impasse.* The 'sharer' had no control over the management of the cultivation or the arrangements for leasing lands, etc., from which his profit was to be derived; the 'gancar' had parted (bit by bit) with every vestige of the income he once derived from the lands (and other sources), which he was nevertheless alone empowered to manage. The landholder with his fixed rent, or his 'lease,' had nothing to say to either. Up to 1735, the *collections under various heads* (sic) were sold by auction to the Gancar (in the village) who made the highest

[1] This is suggested by references to different kinds or classes of income, e.g., '*tangas de gutoga,*' '*tangas de raxy*' (which latter is said to include certain items, as *recamo, vantem, serodio*). It is impossible (and the dictionaries give no help) to find what either these distorted native or the Portuguese words mean. 'Gutta' (or Gutaka) in Marāthi (by the way) means a monopoly or sale, for a fixed annual payment, of a right to certain variable amounts from a given source. 'Raxy' (Rākhi or Rākshi) *might* mean some tax levied for protection of the place against enemies.

bid.[1] A bailiff (*saccador*) was also appointed to go round and collect the actual payments; and *he* got the post (and might be an outsider) as the person who offered the *lowest* bid at auction, i.e. would accept the smallest personal remuneration for the work of collecting. In 1735 the orders (Cap. 3) permitted (at last) that the sharers should be allowed to bid at the (annual) auction, but (to save appearance of altering the rule) *through* a Gancar. Some further changes were made; but not till about 1850 were the 'sharers' allowed any voice in the management. When this was conceded, the 'headmen' as such, having nothing in the way of interest except in their hereditary holdings (and those perhaps much encumbered), ceased to have any distinctive position.[2] In 1858 they petitioned that they might be restored to their former rights. Nothing, however, could be done, and they gradually dropped out of the records, the more recent papers containing no reference to them. Dr. J. N. da Fonseca says expressly "there are now no headmen." Meanwhile efforts were made to reconstitute some kind of 'community' out of the new material—the 'sharers' and others, and the landholders who still had various interests. Some of the sharers held their right in the form of a share in the profits (whatever they might be) in the particular collection in which they had an interest. Others had been able to commute their interest to a cash pension of fixed amount; others held a 'lease' or farm (of certain items of collection) at a fixed sum in perpetuity.

The confusion was enough to puzzle the wisest administrator, and unfortunately the whole had been attempted to be regulated by orders which were drafted and dealt with by European lawyers who evidently possessed little or no knowledge of the village tenures and native customs.

[1] He would then have to account to the various 'sharers' for the money each was entitled to; and if he was fortunate in his bid he would find the actual collections sufficient to satisfy the revenue and the sharers, and have a little over for himself.

[2] Evidently the 'sharers' had to be responsible for the revenue among themselves; or some official saw the revenue payment taken, before the 'sharers' were allowed to touch the balance.

In 1882 the curious experiment was tried of making (by law) the whole body of interested 'sharers' into a kind of joint-stock company. Some, who had fixed 'pensions' (in lieu of profits), retained them; all others had to commute their rights into a certain number of shares of Rs. 10 each (fractions not being allowed). Apparently over a large part of the village lands no separate possessory rights remained.[1] The lands, or rather the dues leviable on them, were the 'capital' of the joint-stock association, *who also owned all the ploughs and tools and cattle.* I have not seen any details as to how the actual cultivation of the land was carried on, and what was the *status* of the persons who worked the fields, whether they paid annual rents or gave a share of the grain, or what. Presumably the rents and other dues of all kinds would be brought to account, the revenue charges first paid and the profits (if any) divided among the pensioners and shareholders.

As might be expected, this plan failed to work; and in 1897 permission was given for the *desamortição* (which I suppose means dissolution) of the joint-stock business, on a resolution of the 'sharers' being passed to that effect. In that case the villages were to be cadastrally surveyed, and the several holdings put up to auction.

We do not possess any details of how this is to be carried out, and it is of course too early to predict results.

But one thing may be confidently stated: the only possible foundation for a permanent arrangement is *to restore* the *raiyatwāri constitution,* i.e. to make a careful cadastral survey, *and to assess on every holding* a proper revenue-demand, which it must pay, without any 'extras' and without any joint-liability. The best plan (if it were not thought impossible) would be to borrow from the Bombay Government (who alone possess the really competent staff) a good Settlement officer and body of experienced land-classifiers to do the work.

[1] What with vacant holdings, the unappropriated rice-lands, the resumed grants, and the escheated lands, the area actually held by hereditary cultivators (with a certain customary assessment to pay) must have become quite a minor portion of the whole area.

The question of the rights of the 'sharers' would have to be settled by commuting uncertain claims for a fixed amount, to be met either by taking over the hereditary right in the (vacant) holdings, or having a certain allowance paid through the treasury, the revenue-demand being adjusted on this supposition. Perhaps certain sharers might be recognized as 'superior occupants' entitled to a (defined) rentcharge on this or that holding or survey number. Thus the villages would return to being orderly 'raiyatwāri' villages, as they were at first. And perhaps some descendants of the old Gāṅwkārs and Kulkarṇis could again take office as headmen and accountants, under proper rules to prevent any right to the emoluments or to the authority becoming again shared among a number, or being frittered away or alienated.

THE ORIGIN OF ZAMINDARI ESTATES IN BENGAL.

THIS paper may at once be described as a short study in the history of the "Permanent Settlement" of Bengal. The administrative and fiscal experiment so denominated is familiar, at least by name, to every reader of Indian history, partly because it necessarily finds a place in any account of the rule of the East India Company in Bengal, partly because it is associated with many (not always reasonable) differences of opinion, and partly, also, because it is understood, in general terms, to have involved the solution of some rather curious economic problems. A concrete illustration of the working of this measure will hardly need any lengthened apology. In order to make such an illustration intelligible, it will be necessary to call to mind exactly what "the settlement" implied; and some of my readers may not object to be reminded, and others to be informed, what it was that Lord Cornwallis did in Bengal in 1793.

For a moment we must go back to the beginning,— to the remote period of the Aryan invasion. The tract of country known in the eighteenth century as "Bengal, Bihar, and Orissa," comprises the eastern end of the great Ganges valley or plain. The northern part was "Bihar," the central and eastern "Bengal"; while "Orissa" meant a south-western portion, now occupied by the district of Midnapore, and including only the upper portion of the east coast province, marked on the maps as "Orissa." The Aryan advance could not have reached this eastern territory till a comparatively long period had elapsed since the tribes first established themselves in "Aryavarta," the tract just east of the Jamna River, whence they gradually extended their dominion, developing all the while that peculiar system of caste, of social polity, religion, philosophy, and law, which we distinguish as Hindu. In modern Bengal the lower orders of the agricultural population at the present day are very largely of the aboriginal *i.e.*, non-Aryan stock. Even the middle castes are of a mixed and much altered race. The purer Aryan or Hindu type is represented by a limited upper social crust, a ruling and everywhere dominant element. The effect of their first domination was to cover the land with a network of kingdoms and chiefships,—small as kingdoms, but in fact comprising considerable areas of land,—each including many hundreds of villages. The Brahman (or priestly) caste converted the whole country, and made it subservient to their system. It became respectable to be in some "caste," however lowly; for below the humblest castemen there are still many "outcaste" races. The military (or Kshatriyā) caste furnished the rulers and chiefs.

For many centuries the Hindu Rajas reigned apparently without oppressing the people, collecting their chief revenue in the form of a share in the grain produce of the land. The subjects who raised the rice and other crops which yielded this revenue were of various agricultural castes; and their holdings were (as usual in level open countries) aggregated in limited groups, which appear to have been of a simple character. There was no joint ownership or holding in common. The "villages" were groups of independent cultivators, descendants of the first clearers of the soil, held together by locality and by common submission to a hereditary headman. Each village had also its own staff of menials and artisans, who furnished all the simple wants of daily life in complete independence of neighboring townships or villages. There were none of those more strongly organized "joint" or landlord villages in which some dominant family or some section of a conquering tribe claims the whole village as a unit estate enjoyed in certain definite shares. There is some reason to believe that in Bihar families (of the Bābhan caste) had at one time obtained the dominion of villages, and held them in this way, but not in Bengal. Perhaps the local Rajas and chiefs did not make many grants which enabled superior families to become landlords of villages. Adventurers were not allowed to make petty conquests and settlements, and the Rajas seem to have maintained a conservative and direct rule over the cultivators. There is no reason to believe that the older Hindu law or polity sanctioned the idea that the king or chief was owner of the soil. Even if called so in the language of Oriental adulation, he did not interfere with the people; and he only appears as taking a share in the produce (fixed by custom at one-sixth, but often raised in times of necessity). He was entitled to levy other customary tolls and taxes, as well as to require certain supplies of food, wood, and fodder. From the earliest times the Raja had also the undisputed right of disposing of unoccupied waste and forest land.

In the fourteenth century of our era the Hindu chiefs were subdued under the Muhammadan kingdom of Bengal, one of the products of the earlier Pathan invasions of India. But this change did not directly affect village life or tenures, except by the occasional and local grant of villages (*i.e.*, of the royal rights in them). When the old Hindu ruler had been slain in battle or driven out, the direct revenue administration simply passed to the Moslem officials. We know that in the fourteenth century the revenue was still taken in kind, though the demand was raised (at least nominally) to one-half the produce. But, as a matter of fact, a number of Rajas and chiefs submitted, and were allowed to take the place of dependent nobles in the Moslem kingdom. In fact, the conquerors were only too glad to conciliate them. It was eminently politic to leave them in the management of the internal affairs of their former kingdoms, allowing them to retain the state and title of Raja on condition of their passing on a share of the revenue to the treasury,—a share which in the course of time was converted into a money payment.

Like other Oriental dynasties, the Bengal royal houses gradually waxed weaker. There was some recovery under Sher Shah, but the complete success of the Mughal dynasty at Delhi in the sixteenth century put an end at last to the independent kingdom of Bengal. The Mughal conqueror had neither racial connection nor actual sympathy with the earlier Pathan moslems. Bengal became a "Sūba" or great province of the Mughal empire, and so remained, in varying degrees of dependence, till the close of the eighteenth century. Akbar took the supreme rule (1576 A.D.), and a few years later the revenue of Bengal was roughly settled by a cash assessment. For many years afterwards the amounts then fixed were observed, and formed the basis on which subsequent rulers proceeded to enhance the rates or to assess newly acquired territories. The last formal settlement was in 1722 A.D. After that, almost yearly changes were made by demand of extra cesses, but there was no new "settlement."

The Mughal empire, however, like all others, in its turn suffered decline; and its effective control over the more distant provinces grew weak. The process may be said to have begun during the last half of Aurangzeb's long reign (A.D. 1658–1707). That unfortunate, if able, monarch was then moved by his evil genius to devote his personal energies to the conquest of the remaining kingdoms of the Dakhan, or southern division of India, a country which nature had separated from "Hindustan" by the hill country of the Vindhya, that great network of ranges which runs across the middle of India on either side of the Narbadā River. In those days of difficult communication, when the headquarters were removed from Agra or Delhi, the emperor's control over the further extremities of the Ganges plain inevitably became somewhat relaxed. The revenues of Bengal had been revised and considerably increased in 1658, under Sultān Shuja', one of the brothers of Aurangzeb, whom the latter had defeated and put to flight. Special arrangements had to be made during the emperor's absence from his capital; and it is understood that what I may at once call the "farming system" of the Bengal revenues was much extended during the latter years of this reign, though it only became universal in 1713. The number of districts for which there were hereditary territorial Rajas and chiefs, such as I have mentioned, was not large; and it was necessary in many places to employ revenue officials, local capitalists, and others, to be responsible for fixed sums from the different districts. The size of the "estates" let in farm in this way varied from a great territory to the small revenue subdivision known as a "pargana." But many of the more successful "farmers," as we shall see, managed to aggregate several smaller farms in their own hands; and estates of very large size were thus built up. Farming of single villages, which was so common in other parts, does not seem to have ever been in favor in Bengal.

District revenue farming having once become an established and universal practice, it seemed to take root in the soil of Bengal, and practically remained unbroken till British rule began. The direct effect of "farming" was gradually to withdraw from the villages such measure of protection as the supervision of the State revenue officers of the districts had been wont to give. In early times the government accounts contained detailed lists of all villages; and the revenue payment from each, according to the last regular assessment, could be checked. There was a hierarchy of officials, from the village accountant

(Patwāri) to the subdivision officer ('Āmil), and from him to the district and provincial authorities. Under the farming system all this detail became unnecessary. The treasury officials henceforth only cared for the comparatively short list of "estates" and the total due from each. The local officials were soon completely atrophied or turned into the mere creatures of the "farmers." They neither could nor would exercise any control over their proceedings. If the farmer raised the demand on the villages or committed extortion on his own account, no one cared. Had a local officer attempted to interfere, he would have failed: the farmer would have had his excuses ready; and the treasury, looking only to the safety of the stipulated total sum, would have sided with the farmer rather than with the officer. I do not mean to give the impression that this abandonment of control came about all at once. When the "farmers" were first employed, the conditions were strict: regular warrants of appointment were issued, and were backed by a recognizance signed by the farmer, accepting various duties and responsibilities.* He was bound to keep detailed accounts, showing the whole of his collections, paying in about nine-tenths and keeping one-tenth (besides certain other allowances of land held free). And these accounts were at first well scrutinized.

The tributary Rajas and other territorial magnates of greater importance were, however, always more or less exempted from this control; and, as others grew in wealth and importance, they were increasingly left alone. And, though the warrants (*sanad*) were still issued, the matter became very much one of bargain for a fixed sum, and no questions asked as to how it was raised or how much more the farmer got for himself. In time the distinction

* For the forms, etc., of appointment, see my *Land Systems of British India*, vol. i. p. 511, and Hunter's *Bengal Records*, vol. i. p. 37, ff. The Zamindar was responsible for the peace and security of the district, for the post-office, and for communications, bridges, and embankments (in the flooded districts).

of origin of the different classes of farmers was forgotten, and all were alike spoken of as "Zamīndār." The term means "holder of the land," but technically refers to the control of the aggregate of the royal rights in the lands which were made over to the manager against a fixed money payment.

The Zamindars and their agents were naturally brought much closer to the land than the governors or the official classes could be. In fact, they conducted themselves as if they were perpetual lessees of all the State rights. But in the course of time a change had come over the relations of the ruler to the land, which had an important bearing on the growth of the Zamindar's position. I have already mentioned that early Hindu law knew nothing of any claim of the sovereign to be owner of all land; nor indeed does the strict Muhammadan law countenance such a theory. But the result of repeated conquests and of the revolts and assertions of independent rule that make up so large a part of Indian history was that (at an uncertain period) the sovereigns began to claim, and to exercise the claim, to be owners of every acre of land in their dominions. More cannot here be said on the subject. But, certainly by the end of the eighteenth century, every ruler of a kingdom, whether Hindu or Moslem, had established his claim to general ownership, and the claim had stood for some generations at least. And this extended meaning, the "Zamindāri" right of the State, naturally enabled the assignees, or "Zamindars," to enlarge their pretensions. They acquired by prescriptive right a control which was virtually that of owner, although no formal assertion could be made that the ruler in assigning the usufruct had parted with the actual ownership.

One further element in the case deserves a word of notice. A large part of every estate consisted of waste land; the Zamindar was undoubtedly entitled to bring this under cultivation, and was not required to increase his total contract-payment in consequence of so doing. Hence the new cultivated land was virtually his own; and, as he located his own laborers on this new cultivation, they really were his "tenants" on the basis of contract.

In 1765 the East India Company obtained the grant of the civil and revenue administration of "Bengal, Bihār, and Orissa." They were to pay a fixed tribute to the Delhi treasury, to be responsible for all expenditure, and to take the local revenue. When the British officers assumed the task of administration, they found the whole country — that is, the settled and cultivated districts — divided up into "Zamindāris" of one kind or another. The villages had become mere bodies of tenants under the Zamindars: all effective independent right of the communities had long disappeared. It is not surprising that the officials of a mercantile company were at first unable to deal effectively with such a state of affairs. Their staff was organized on a commercial footing; and they could do no more than try to supervise the native system, and gradually improve their position, changing, in fact, from "writers" and "merchants" to district officers and governors. But the native system was so rotten that as early as 1772 an attempt at direct administration had to be made. Still, "farming" the revenue in one form or other was the only possible plan. Attempts were made now to fix quinquennial terms, now to have annual contracts. But this, though promising a more direct control over the farmers, proved a source of injustice. No discrimination was possible, except in a few cases, between the real hereditary "Zamindars" and the other classes. Many of the former would not consent to take the place of mere annual contractors with no other rights beyond what their contract gave them; and many persons who for generations had acquired rights, however ill defined, were consequently ousted altogether.

When the Company's charter had to be renewed (every twenty years), the statute book shows that the renewal was accompanied by an act of Parliament intended to introduce reforms and to guarantee good government. The first act of this kind which attempted seriously to deal with the land question in Bengal was Pitt's India act of 1784 (24 Geo. III.). By this time the authorities in India had made some progress in organizing their official staff; and, in particular, there had been a useful reconstruction by which the Bengal "Board of Revenue" had been separated from the general Executive Council. Corresponding changes in the district administrative staff had been made. A good deal might be said about the act of 1784, and what it was really intended to do,—a matter which has often been misunderstood. Here I must be content shortly to say that the result was the sending out of Lord Cornwallis as governor-general, with John Shore as his adviser. They sailed in 1786,* with a detailed despatch (dated April 12, 1786) giving instructions as to how the act was to be carried out. The instructions were to devise a system which should be "permanent"; that is, not liable to annual or quinquennial changes. And, though a suggestion was made that a "perpetual" assessment was to be desired, it was ordered that at first a "settlement" for ten years should be made. At the same time justice was to be done by an inquiry into the true position and rights of the Zamindars, so that those who had been ousted unfairly might be restored.

Had the "land revenue" been a mere tax, so much per acre of land according to value, the task of assessing it would have been a purely fiscal one. It could have been

* Sir John Shore, afterwards Lord Teignmouth, and himself governor-general in succession to Lord Cornwallis, became president of the Board of Revenue, and applied himself to a study of the Bengal revenue system. He acquired as real an insight into it as was possible in those days. His Minutes of 1788–89 are masterpieces of detailed research and clear exposition.

accomplished without any reference to the legal position or the rights of the people who held the land. But such a view of the matter was impossible under the circumstances. No kind of maps or survey data existed: the area of the cultivated land could only be guessed at; and even the boundaries of the Zamindari estates were only described in words, and that in the vaguest manner. It is doubtful whether in the palmy days of Mughal rule more than a very rough and partial measurement of village lands had been made (*circa* 1582 A.D.). Such a record could be of little value, even if it had been much more detailed than it was, after two hundred years had elapsed, when the area had increased by subsequent acquisitions, and the revenue itself had been much raised. It was obvious, under the circumstances, that it would be useless to fix the revenue demand without determining what persons were to be held responsible for it, and what legal position the payers were to have, since under any organized system of government no one could be responsible for the revenue without a definite understanding of his powers and position in relation to the land and to the subordinate landholders from whom the amounts must ultimately be raised. In short, it was necessary to find the proper engagees first, and then discuss with them the amount to be paid. No other basis of assessment was possible, in the absence of a survey and valuation of lands, than a consideration of the average amount of past collections. And then, under this new system, it was evident that the Zamindars would no longer be required to manage the police or to pay pensions or control the excise and other such matters, so that very considerable adjustments of the payments from each farm and the deductions to be made, would be requisite.

By this time, even if the Act and the executive despatch had been less explicit than they were, no doubt could be entertained that the Zamindars were the proper persons, in most cases, to make the settlement with. But how was their legal position to be defined? The government found itself the legal successor of the native power, and *de facto* paramount owner of the soil. It is probable that Lord Cornwallis and his advisers believed, further, that the State right was not only *de facto*, but also *de jure*. If government, then, was the owner, the Zamindar was not; and what should he be called? Lord Cornwallis had no difficulty in coming to the determination that the government should not retain the right to cultivated or occupied land. This he did, not on historic or legal grounds, but as a matter of public policy. The Zamindars (with other minor holders in a similar position) seemed to be the only possible candidates for the grant of the landlord title. This, however, raised a controversy, because the various origins of the whole class of Zamindars had become forgotten. Some writers asserted that all alike were official appointments connected with the farming of the revenue: others insisted on the hereditary character of some of them, and their long connection with the soil as Rajas. Both sides generalized from the particular facts to which they directed their attention, and extended their views to cover the whole case.* There can hardly be any doubt that, if existing conditions required the selection of "landlords" to take over the ownership of which the government wished to divest itself, the Zamindars had the best claim. Although theoretically this claim was more historical and real in the case of the old Rajas, like Bishnupur and others, who, though not

* It is curious to notice how the late M. de Laveleye (*Propriété Primitive*, p. 117) represents the matter. Not only does he generalize in one the whole class of Bengal landlords, but he treats the case as one with that of the Oudh Talukdar landlords; and he speaks of a single *article de loi* under which, as he supposes, by a few strokes of the legislative pen, revenue-farmers were turned into landlords. Yet the Oudh Talukdars were not dealt with till sixty-five years after the Permanent Settlement, in a different province, and under a wholly different law, and at a time when the policy was completely changed, and officials were extremely anxious to deal with the villages direct.

territorial chiefs, had yet enjoyed a very long possession, it was equally true that a practical prescription of some generations could be asserted in favor of the local men of wealth, and even of the hereditary officials who had long been employed as Zamindars.

One of the points that I shall hope to illustrate presently is how these great men who were *not* originally territorial rulers grew up and acquired estates. But, assuming the claims of the Zamindars, the difficulty was by no means at an end; for what was to be the position of the village cultivators? When once the government began to determine the difficult question of private rights in the soil,* it was clearly necessary to determine the question all through,—to deal both with the superior and the subordinate right. Lord Cornwallis's proclamation of 1793 vests the landlord right in the Zamindars and other "actual proprietors," and it is sometimes supposed that the question of inferior rights was shirked. But there was nothing of the kind. The law dealt first with certain subordinate holders and managers and grantees on fixed rentals, some of whom were, or ought to be, independent of the Zamindars. These were all made direct landlords or proprietors, and the class need not engage our attention further. When the grade of actual village cultivators was reached, there was no intention of leaving them unprotected; but the authorities did not really know what was necessary. They thought they were

* Indeed, this necessity could not long have been evaded under any method of treatment. If government had retained its own paramount ownership of the soil, the rights of the Zamindars (whatever they were) could never have been settled by the courts of law; for no analogy or legal principle could have been found to guide their decision. Legislation alone could have solved the difficulty. When, on the other hand, government resolved to renounce the ownership, it obviously was incumbent on it to say to whom the ownership was transferred or who was to be recognized as enjoying it. No one could have thought in those days of restoring the village cultivators to a full proprietary or independent position which had been lost for generations; nor is it probable that any system of management such as is now in use in Southern India would have been successful or even possible.

taking practical and sufficient action by doing two things. First, they enacted by law that the landlords must give the village "tenants" definite written "pottahs," specifying what the rent was; and they prohibited under severe penalty the exaction of anything more, declaring their conviction that the tenants would then be perfectly safe.* The landlords, they supposed, grateful for the benefits secured to them, would in their turn foster their tenants, and feel it their own best policy to extend the favors they had received, to them. And, second, government reserved the power at any time to make laws and regulations to protect the rights of the tenants.

It would be impossible here even to indicate the reasons why the first measure proved altogether illusory; but it may be mentioned that the root of the whole difficulty was that government never definitely determined whether the Zamindars could or could not enhance the cultivator's payments, which now became the "rent" payable to the middlemen landlords. In some cases of privileged tenancy the matter was obvious; but as regards the whole class of resident villagers not located by the Zamindar himself, there was much doubt. Out of the second reservation arose the possibility of the subsequent tenant legislation of 1859 and 1885.

* The vernacular term "pottah" (*pattā*) is the best, for nothing exactly like it exists under Western law. It was not a lease: it was rather a note of the amount of rent and other terms of tenure, which did not necessarily *create the title to hold*, as a lease does.

It will be remembered that in Bengal (and in other parts of India) the favorite method of getting an increase was not openly to raise the rate, but to levy an extra cess (*abwāb*), on one pretext or another; and this, once imposed, was never taken off. The old government had adopted this plan with the Zamindars themselves. Thus, when the Marathas threatened Bengal, the government imposed a cess, called "Chauth-Marhatta," to meet the composition they had to pay for immunity from attack. The Zamindars followed the example by not only demanding the amount from their tenants, but adding many like "cesses" for their own benefit. See my *Land Systems*, vol. i. p. 419, for detailed examples of the curious and varied pretexts on which these cesses were levied. Each bore its own name, according to the occasion of it (real or fancied).

Thus the "Permanent Settlement" involved several points. (1) The abandonment (locally) by the State of its ownership of the soil. (2) The conferment of the proprietorship, subject to whatever necessary restrictions, on some persons held best entitled on the ground of long prescriptive possession, however obtained originally. (3) The protection of the cultivating classes under the landlords. (4) The adjustment of the amount of the revenue payable annually in certain instalments by the landlords, and the powers of the State to secure itself from default in the payments. (5) Lastly, there was the question, For how long should the assessment hold good? It is in consequence of this variety of the necessary operations that several interesting points have arisen concerning land taxation, tenant right, and other matters, which have been of value as practical lessons for other parts of India, and are not devoid of interest in other countries.

Accounts of this settlement, more or less in detail, are now easily accessible. But they necessarily deal with the subject in the abstract, and refer to the various minutes recorded and to the Regulations.* What, however, is not so common is to find concrete illustrations of the actual growth and origin of estates, and of the effect of the settlement on them. A great deal of light of this kind has been thrown on the subject by the publication of Sir W. W. Hunter's abstracts of the principal correspondence of the Board of Revenue during the first twenty-five years after its organization in 1781. But the use of such materials is almost confined to those who can obtain access to the entire documents or who have local knowledge suffi-

*Up to 1834 the enactments of the Calcutta legislature were officially called "Regulations." Thus the law of the Permanent Settlement is contained in Regulations I. of 1793 and VIII. of the same year, with, of course, many other subsidiary enactments.

cient to enable them to understand the abstract. It happened, however, that in the years immediately following the settlement the government formed a plan of collecting statistical information about the condition of the country and its inhabitants, and about the climate, crops, and natural productions of the several districts. Dr. Buchanan-Hamilton * was a medical officer in the service of the government; and in those days — indeed, long after — the medical officers were the only people who had any knowledge of botany and other natural sciences, such as was requisite in drawing up the reports contemplated. He had made in 1800–1, a tour over Mysore, Malabar, and the Southern Presidency, the narrative of which was published in London (3 vols., 1807). In 1807 and following years he submitted reports on the Bengal districts, and twenty-five folio volumes of manuscript still remain in the India Office. They have been made use of in various early works on India, but were never printed *in extenso*. In 1832 arrangements were made to print some of the reports, from the Calcutta Office copy, in a magazine issued in connection with the Asiatic Society of Bengal. Only one volume appeared, in 1838, relating to the district of Dinājpur.† Having had occasion to go through this in some detail, I was struck by the light it threw on three rather interesting topics: the origin of (one class of) "Zamindar's" estates; the nature of the assessment and its effects; and, third, the condition of the "tenants" within ten years after the confirmation of the settlement. Dr. Hamilton was not acquainted with the details of the regulation law or the revenue procedure. He was, however, a shrewd and, on the whole, an accurate as well as a careful observer; and

* He was first known as Buchanan, but afterwards took the name of Hamilton. I refer to him by the latter name for the sake of brevity.

† A district in Central Bengal lying some way almost due north of Calcutta between 24° and 26° north latitude.

the absence of technical knowledge on his part renders his recorded observations all the more interesting, as showing the facts uncolored by reference to official and professional views. He knew nothing of land tenures or their history, and approached the subject entirely from the point of view common at the time. The existence of a landlord, and the idea that every one cultivating the fields under such a landlord must be a contract-tenant pure and simple,—this appears to him the natural and necessary order of things, as it would to most English writers of the eighteenth and early nineteenth centuries. Dr. Hamilton is no opponent of the form of settlement adopted. He has no prejudices against the "Zamindar" class. He finds them lamentably deficient, but he finds equal fault with the tenants. He discusses no abstract principles, and has none of that partisan spirit which seems to take possession of some of our early writers on land questions. He simply notes what he observed, and comments on it. His account of the Dinajpur estates is, then, trustworthy and instructive.

Sir W. Hunter has, I think, fairly satisfactorily grouped the Zamindars under four heads of origin.* (1) There were the old territorial Rajas, who had once been independent rulers, had been recognized as tributary chiefs under the Moslem rule, and, by the gradual growth of the claims of the rulers and chiefs on the soil, had become virtual landlords. Their interest, in fact, dated back before the Mughal conquest in 1576. (2) There were great landholders, some of whom had acquired the title of Raja. Indeed, some of them were chiefs or rulers of their territories, only of less ancient date than the first class. (3) There were real "farmers," who were allowed to manage tracts of country from father to son, so that they had a distinctly hereditary position, and had held

* *Bengal Records*, vol. i. p. 31.

for some generations (at least for nearly a century). (4) There were modern farmers and managers under the British government since 1765, but who had in some instances a continuous prescriptive position up to 1793.

It is the second class that the Dinajpur district illustrates, or perhaps the third; for it is not easy to draw a definite line between the two. The district was found to be divided into a number of local areas separately named, and called "parganas." I cannot discover the origin of this, except that it does not (positively) appear that they were the areas of which different tribes or clans had once taken possession.* And in Hamilton's time these parganas were closely connected with revenue-farming. As one person would farm one, two, or more, and then sell or partition them, the number was liable to change. There were ninety-eight parganas in 1807. As the local names are of no interest to the non-Indian reader, I will allude to them where necessary by the serial number they bear on the list. Out of this total number, sixty-one belonged at the date of the settlement to one Dinajpur estate, which thus covered the larger part, but not the whole, of the district. The estate and the family that possessed it were the growth apparently of about a century and a quarter before the settlement.†

Somewhere about 1660 a person named Kāsi obtained the farm of the revenues of six parganas. Nothing is known of this person except that he was a Brahman. It is not suggested that he had any hereditary land in the place. His widow was allowed to succeed him, and then some friend of hers, for whom she solicited the appoint-

* Which is a common origin of such divisions in other parts of Northern India.

† This is instructive, because we are continually hearing of the supposed antiquity of tenures, and about lands "held for ninety generations," and the like. As Dr. Hamilton remarks, "From the total want of history among the Hindus, any custom which has obtained for a hundred years comes to them with its origin as obscure as if it had been a thousand."

ment from Srimanta, the "Chief Kanungo" of Bengal.* After this the official thought he would like the farm himself, and took possession. On his death his son succeeded jointly with an adopted son. This shows that either the "Zamindari" was already hereditary (this must have been during Aurangzeb's reign) or that the office of Kanungo was. The adopted son (Sukhdev by name) was the energetic one of the family. He added to the estate by becoming manager or agent for a neighboring Zamindar, and, on the death of this person, annexing the estate. He now applied for and received the title of "Raja." His son Prān-nāth continued the work of expanding the estate, and under him or his near successors the whole of the parganas of the farm were got together. "He lived in great splendor, and was a very great oppressor in his neighborhood, seizing on all the small Zamindaris near him, partly by force, partly by corruption." Inscriptions bearing his name from 1704 to 1733 A.D. are found. He had no son, but adopted one Rāmnāth. This person continued the same course, and had such a number of followers that the governor (Subadār) of Bengal treated him with great leniency, and gave him the title of "Maharaja." He was allowed to farm the land-revenue of the whole district for the very low sum of 463,000 rupees annually.† He lived till A.D. 1754. The family was now titled, so they adopted the rule of primogeniture; and the eldest son in future succeeded alone to the title and estate.

A rapid sketch of the steps in the acquisition of the parganas which constituted the estate may now be given.

* *Kanungo* (or *Qanungo*) means one who declares (*go*) the rule (*qānun* = *canon*) in revenue matters. He knows the rules and practice, and supervises the accountants and petty officers. There was one in each district, and a chief officer over the whole province.

† See Mr. Grant's *Analysis of the Finances of Bengal*, printed in the *Fifth Report on the Affairs of the East India Company* (presented to Parliament 1812). Reprint of 1883, vol. i. p. 261. For some subsequent (small) increases, see *ibid.*, pp. 296, 320.

The numbers 1–6 were the original grant to Kāsi, as above stated. No particulars of numbers 7–28 were known. Number 29 was purchased. Here we see how a right over the land is beginning to be asserted; for the *office* of farmer could not, in the nature of things, be properly sold. And long afterwards (under the company's government) we find official objection taken to Zamindars selling the lands under their control. Number 30 had been held by a Brahman, on whose death Raja Ramnath had seized the "estate," the relations of the late owner declaring that they had been kept in confinement for many years, and at last had been bought off with a small subsistence pension. Numbers 31 and 32 were said to have belonged to some collateral relations of the chief Qanungo, above mentioned; and the first Raja of Dinajpur forcibly ejected them. Number 33 was only shared (with some other person) by the Dinajpur Zamindar. Number 34 was "acquired," but the way is not stated. Number 35 was seized in war against the chief who held it by the Dinajpur Raja in alliance with another chief. The victors divided the spoils. Then follow several parganas in which only shares had been bought or seized. Then, again, numbers 42–60 formed a large estate of a Khatri * family, which, as so often occurs in the higher families, came to be left without an heir, when the estate was dismembered, and the family of Sukhdev (above mentioned) got a considerable portion. Number 61 was acquired in part by the Dinajpur family standing security for the revenue dues of the owner, and taking the land when he failed to pay. Many of these events must have happened before the actual decline of the Mughal empire, showing how little the outlying provinces, and especially Bengal, were under effective control.

So much for the Dinajpur estate: it came under the settlement in 1786, and was confirmed, like the rest, in

* The trading and banking caste.

1793. In the course of a few years, as is often the case with unwieldy estates, it fell into the hands of bad agents and managers, so that default was made, and the whole was sold for arrears of revenue. The estate was thus broken up. But the descendants of the family still retain a considerable area of land; for they saved a portion of the original property, and afterwards repurchased some of the "lots."

A few words may be added as to the other thirty-seven parganas which belonged to other "Zamindars" of the same origin. One important estate was that of Shām Rai and Rām Rai (brothers) in the "Sirkār" (Muhammadan district) of Tājpur. "Several forts and ruins," says Dr. Hamilton, "attest their former consequence." The estate was divided between two families. The first division descended for some generations to the then (1807) Zamindar, whose education had been neglected, and who had an equally ill-informed estate manager. "They are in the hands of kites who in a few years will probably ruin their affairs." The other division passed to a family who already had other possessions in the east part of the district, and became partitioned among the family.

Another estate was a pargana (number 77) given as a present by the Dinajpur Raja to Ganga Govind-Singha, the diwān * of the East India Company under Warren Hastings. Number 78 formed another estate made up of contributions of land from all the neighboring Zamindaris. Doubtless, this was given as a douceur or as hush money for Kantha Babu, private diwan to Warren Hastings. The pargana so made up contained two hundred and forty villages, or "mauza."

Another considerable estate (number 81 with 83 and part of 84) deserves mention, as it originated in a grant of waste land under the Emperor Jahāngīr (A.D. 1605–27),

* A minister of State; or, in private estates, a superintendent or manager, such as would be a land agent in England.

and was gradually established, and then added to.* After some curious transactions, which Dr. Hamilton did not feel sure about, the estate came to be divided between four branch-families. They were Brahmans, but nearly illiterate. "They would be totally destitute of any appearance of literature, had they not been taught by rote a few verses of Songskrito (Sanskrit), and informed of their meaning. . . . They seem to pass their time chiefly in sleeping, eating, picking their teeth, and other such recreations, or in listening to singers and story-tellers, and very rarely go out of the house."

Only one more instance must be cited as illustrating the manners of the time. The parganas numbers 87 and 88 formed part of an immense estate which was granted by the Subadār Ja'fir Khān' (Nawāb, or native governor, of Bengal) to a Brahman who had rendered him an important service; namely, that of treacherously giving up the registrar-general's (Qanungo's) seal, which was in his keeping, and affixing it to certain revenue accounts of the Subadar, which the chief Qanungo had refused to pass. It will be observed from this that in Ja'fir Khan's time (A.D. 1704–25) the governor of Bengal was still in some awe of the head of the revenue officials, who could report to the imperial treasury at Delhi.

Such an origin for landlord estates as these examples indicate is by no means uncommon, and is certainly not confined to Dinajpur. But, after a century, irregularities, and even violence and fraud, are forgotten, and a prescriptive title in the hands of the present holder is all that appears. In 1793 the Dinajpur Raja was probably a wealthy and dignified person, quite ignorant of the deeds of his predecessors; and, just as probably, he would have been ready to assert that his ancestors had held the land from

* Here, of course, there would be a good foundation for a real proprietary title, as the waste always belonged to the State (whatever other land did); and, being uncultivated, it was free for the grantee to own and to settle his own (contract) tenants on.

time immemorial. It is quite clear, indeed, that many years before 1793 the virtually landlord character of the "Zamindari" had become practically established, and the "estate" was acknowledged as hereditary, and even transferable. Indeed, Dr. Hamilton was told it had been so always; but this is certainly not historically true. From the earlier transactions in the list above given, it is evident that, though a son often succeeded the father, the revenue authorities of those days never hesitated about taking away the "estate," and giving it to any one they pleased. Consistency or respect for legal principle is not to be looked for in the revenue administration of the later days of the empire.

Dr. Hamilton remarks, however, on the then existing "position" of the Zamindars,—*i.e.*, since the Permanent Settlement,—and that "they have been placed exactly on the footing of the landlords of England" (which is far from being legally correct), "except that the land tax is higher; but, then, they are exempt from almost all others." It is interesting also to note that fourteen years after the Permanent Settlement the parties on whom so valuable a source of wealth had been conferred were totally unappreciative of its advantages; and this solely because there was a condition for punctual payment of the land revenue, and a stringent law of sale in case of default. It is true that these payments, as fixed by the settlement of 1793, were, just for the time being, higher than what the Zamindars had been obliged to pay to the ill-supported and disorganized native State. "They said," concludes Dr. Hamilton, "that formerly they were allowed great authority, both in criminal and civil causes, over the people whom they managed (which was a great source of emolument, being of course venally administered); and, although they were often squeezed by the Mughal officers, and on all occasions treated with the utmost contempt, they preferred suffering these evils to the mode which has been adopted,—of selling their lands when they fall into arrears, which is a practice they cannot endure.* Besides, bribery went a great way on most occasions, and they allege that, bribes included, they did not actually pay one-half of what they do now, although nothing can be more moderate than the present assessment, which I am convinced does not amount to a tithe of the produce."

The last remark naturally leads to the subject of the valuation of the estates, and the mode in which the annual sum (payable in instalments) was determined. The amount, it will be remembered, was ordered to be fixed for ten years; but, when this was done, Lord Cornwallis pressed the home authorities to make the settlement perpetual, and obtained their consent to do so. It was always the rule that, if default was allowed to occur, the Collector would put up such part of the estate as would probably yield the amount to auction sale. I may note, in passing, that it has been a misfortune for Bengal —the rule never obtained in Northern Madras, where there is also a Permanent Settlement—that, when lands under Permanent Settlement are sold for arrears, the purchaser is also entitled to take the estate on the same (permanent) assessment, although he is at liberty to revise the rents of ordinary tenants, being entitled to avoid all such leases and encumbrances created by the defaulter as are not expressly saved by the terms of the law.† It

* The sale laws were from the very first deemed a necessary condition, for the government naturally insisted on punctual payment in return for its own many and valuable concessions. So far as Dinajpur was concerned, the assessment was so easy that no landholder with the slightest pretensions to energy or capacity for management need have been in a moment's danger of not being able to pay his instalments under any ordinary conditions. In other parts of Bengal the revenue was (at first) a full assessment,—as a *permanent* valuation had every reason to be,—but nowhere was it such as could not be punctually discharged. It has since, of course, grown to be extremely light. This was expected and always intended, at least in principle; though the actual rapid growth in the value of land and its produce could hardly have been foreseen.

† Otherwise, of course, a fraudulent person might raise all the money he could, and then purposely default and go off with what he had got, leaving

was, I suppose, at first feared that, if this were not so, no one would be found to bid for the land at the auction. But I see no reason why government, when it revises the sale laws, should not now enact a rule that, if a permanent settled estate has to be sold for arrears, the government will not necessarily grant the purchaser the same assessment, but an equitable one, for such term of years as the ordinary settlement rules allow. Obviously, it would not be possible to touch the Regulation of 1793 as regards its promise of permanency to all the original holders and their descendants and voluntary assigns; but, if the estates are allowed by default to pass away from the natural representative of the original settlement holder, there is no reason why the same terms should be granted to a new-comer. If no one would purchase under such terms, so much the better: let the new settlement be made with the actual cultivator.

But to return to Dinajpur. It is curious how very little information is available for Bengal generally as to the manner in which the assessments were actually made for the ten-year settlement which became permanent. The formal rules are preserved in Colebrooke's *Supplement;* but that work is not easy to obtain, and the rules do not explain much as regards the actual practice. The *Fifth Report* disposes of the whole subject in a few lines.* In most parts there was a record of the former collections, and it was ascertained how much belonged to land-revenue proper, other items, such as toll and tax and excise, being separately dealt with. There were various adjustments to be made, which I must pass by entirely, merely noting that the final result was to fix a lump sum for the whole estate, which was a rough estimate, and, in fact, dependent very much on a kind of bargain. Where,

the land so burdened by mortgages, improper leases, and other obligations as to be worthless.

* Reprint of 1883, vol. i. p. 22.

however, such records did not exist, as in Bihar, the rules directed the produce of land to be considered, and a fraction of its calculated annual value to be taken. This seems to have been done in the form of calculating a rough money rate per bīgha (the Bengal bīgha is one-third of an acre). Thus, in Dinajpur in 1786, the Collector (Mr. Hatch) counted up the arable lands in the then existing (98) parganas, and, roughly estimating the amount of one-crop or two-crop land in each, and considering the latter as double the value of the former, took out a general valuation rate per bigha. This brought the assessment total to no more than 1,750,000 rupees. The Collector had nothing to guide him in the way of records of former assessments. Dr. Hamilton does not seem to have been aware of what Mr. Grant's *Analysis* informs us; namely, that shortly before British rule the Dinajpur Maharaja had got such influence that he was allowed to farm the *whole district* for 463,000 rupees, or about one-fourth of the very moderate assessment afterwards made by Mr. Hatch. In 1786, it will be remembered, the Dinajpur estate did not cover the whole district; and, of the above-mentioned 17½ lakhs, the Dinajpur *estate* only accounted for 13½ lakhs.*

As to the moderation of the demand (on the whole district) Dr. Hamilton estimates that there were in 1807 some 6,523,500 bighas (2,174,500 acres) paying government revenue: the rental value to the landlords could not be less than 10 anas per bigha, which would come to fully 4,077,190 rupees, or, with a (very moderate) addition for profits from pasture, fruits, etc., 4,100,000.† Of

* The lākh, or "lac," is 100,000 rupees. Dr. Hamilton could not understand why the Dinajpur estate agent complained of being hardly dealt with, because, apparently, he did not know the facts stated in the text. No doubt the assessment was very easy; but the agent could not forget that once they had been allowed to hold at a mere nominal figure, which of course they could not expect to retain forever, but regretted, nevertheless.

† In 1872 the rates of rent varied from 0.12 to 1.2 rupees in the lowest class,

course, the real income by merely decent management and by extending cultivation, could be progressively raised threefold at least. If that is so, the assessment (17½ lakhs) represents less than 5 anas a bigha, which is decidedly low.

Nevertheless, when Dr. Hamilton came to get the actual figures for some lands (which he confesses were very badly managed lands) still held by the Dinajpur estate, he found out why it was that the Zamindars made, or declared they made, so little net profit. The Zamindar in the old days had been obliged to undertake the duty of maintaining a militia, which was to join the army in war, and perform local quasi-police duties at other times; and he obtained large areas of land exempted from revenue payment in order to support this force. Under the Permanent Settlement he was relieved of this obligation; but the militia still lingered on with no specific duty, and ate up the produce of a number of holdings in the estate. It seems incredible that the landlords instead of dismissing the force, providing for it in the regular police, and utilizing the remainder as bailiffs, actually allowed them to remain on in idleness, and entertained another large staff of "barkandāz" employed to carry messages, enforce distraints, collect payments, and the like. For example, the Dinajpur estate (having, as I said, been broken up shortly after the conclusion of the settlement) consisted in 1807 of some 9 parganas. Of these, 8 (that had been repurchased at auction sales) had a rental of 110,000 rupees. But no less than 7,372 bighas were held rent free (which meant a loss of about 5,000 rupees, at a low computation) for the support of a perfectly useless army of 200 "paiks," with 16 inferior and 24 superior officers of the "older militia," besides

and from 6 to 7.2 rupees in the highest, so that even in 1807 an *all-round* rental rate of 10 anas a bigha (1.14 rupees an acre) was very moderate as a basis of estimating profits.

24 recent employees, with 8 petty officers. And, as if this was not enough, 200 "kutwāls," or messengers, were entertained besides. The whole was supervised by a "diwān" on 100 rupees a month (nominally), with 8 assistants at 25 a month each, 40 "writers," and 16 office-keepers.* And yet all this enormous staff could not manage the rent collections. They were supplemented by a number of rent-farmers, who were responsible for certain portions of the estate, on a commission of 4 per cent. No wonder that, after paying the revenue, there was only a profit of about 15½ per cent. on the gross rental. Though even then there would be other profits from "cesses," wild produce, fruit, and so on. This, of course, is rather an extreme case; but many others were not much better.

The estates were also wretchedly mismanaged, because the actual proprietors, or Zamindars, never controlled their agents or farmers, nor attempted to check their villanies; nor did they interest themselves in the tenants, and see whether they were well-to-do or otherwise. "A great part of them," writes Dr. Hamilton, "never pass the threshold of their doors, except to assist at some religious ceremony, and are either sunk in a miserable superstition, a prey to religious mendicants and other idle persons, or are totally abandoned to dissipation; and some are addicted to both vices." There were, of course, exceptions to be found; and then, especially on the smaller estates,† cultivation was good and the profit large.

Dr. Hamilton had evidently no idea that a village organization once existed in Bengal. He speaks quite complacently of the landlords "judiciously" turning out

* Salaries in India are and always have been paid monthly.

† There can hardly be any doubt that, though the wholesale disruption of the great estates of 1793, owing to failure to pay the revenue, was felt as a hardship at the time, the substitution of a vastly increased number of smaller estates was advantageous to the country. The smaller estates were better managed, and modern legislation has greatly improved the position of tenants.

the "mandal," or headman, of villages, and keeping only the "patwāri," or accountant. He regards both as mere local farmers of rents or servants of the landlord, not as hereditary officers, parts of an ancient and once flourishing social system.

I have alluded to the earliest effect of the sale laws in breaking up the originally settled estates when they failed to pay their revenue. The natural result was that a number of new and smaller estates were formed under new landlords. "The greater part of the (present) landholders," wrote Dr. Hamilton, "are now men who have purchased their estates within these few years, and who formerly were either merchants, manufacturers, agents of landholders, or officers of government. . . . By those natives who are not afraid of them, they are called '*lotdār*,' or fellows who have purchased 'lots,' and are held in great contempt; while there is a general clamor against their rapacity and injustice." It was observed, however, that, even if inclined to be hard, they were much better managers than the old family proprietors, who did nothing and cared nothing. Their lands were in general better cultivated, "and the appearance of the people (tenants) not so miserable as on some of the estates that have belonged to one family for some generations." * On the other hand, Dr. Hamilton speaks strongly of the evil effects of excessive subdivision of land, consequent on the law or custom of joint inheritance. Only in titled families does the custom of primogeniture prevail. In all others the estate is divided and again divided at each succession.

At the present day (taking the published statistics of

* The older families, he goes on to say, were more respected; and people would submit with patience to many things from them as a power to which they were accustomed, that would grieve them to endure from a person of whom they knew nothing or whom they once remembered to have been their equal. The new estate holders were nearly always non-resident, partly owing to their unpopularity.

1872) there are 79 parganas, containing 779 estates or holdings. Only one of these is really large,—88,000 acres; and as many as 238 pay less than 100 rupees per annum. The present revenue (owing to changes in the district area) stands at 1,734,000 rupees. It is remarkable that so completely had the various landholders whose origin has been above sketched absorbed all former rights in the soil that Hunter's *Statistical Account* * informs us how, with a cultivated area of over two million acres, nearly all tenants are now tenants at will: only about one in five will have rights of occupancy; and "fixed rents" (in perpetuity) are rare. While Dr. Hamilton's account applies to a state of things existing more than eighty years ago, it still has its value for the present day. No doubt many changes have taken place; but the want of personal control, the subjection of the tenantry, and many other evils, still continue, at least locally. A certain number of great landlords, no doubt, set a good example; † but, as a rule, the smaller estates are better managed.

I may conclude with a few remarks on the condition of tenants in Dinajpur. Nothing struck me more than the manner in which the purely tenant position of the cultivators was accepted by Dr. Hamilton. Nowhere does he give the least suggestion of a doubt whether a number of the resident village cultivators, who must have existed when the parganas were bought, sold, seized, and granted in the way he describes, had not independent hereditary rights in the soil antecedent to those of the Zamindars, and based on no kind of contract with them. But, in fact, the position of virtual tenancy, so long as it

* The *Statistical Account of Bengal* in twenty volumes.

† Especially when, during a minority, government officers (under the "Court of Wards") have had charge of the estate for a number of years, during which they have had a complete survey and records prepared and a regular rent settlement, by which the tenants have been contented and the coffers of the estate greatly benefited.

was accompanied by no disturbance of actual possession, had very long been acquiesced in. Nevertheless, Dr. Hamilton mentions the fact that the "tenants" always refused to accept leases which were not "perpetual." I am not sure what he means by this. It has been already explained that, in adjusting the new legal order of rights in land, the government believed that every needful legal security for the subordinate "tenants" would be obtained if only the grant of a written lease, or "pottah" (stating the rent payable), was made compulsory; and I suspect that what the author meant was that many cultivators, being really the old original landholders, refused to take "pottahs," unless worded so as to acknowledge a perpetual tenure, or, at all events, so as not to imply that the holding was terminable after a specified number of years.

It is also remarkable that, as regards rates of rent, though the Zamindars had no hesitation in demanding all sorts of "māngan," or irregular levies and benevolences, they at first admitted, in theory, the principle that the "rent" demandable from the old resident (village) tenants was to be calculated at the same rate as that employed in fixing the amount of the government revenue payable by the landlord.* The agents of the landlords assumed that each tenant-holding contained a certain portion of one-crop and a certain portion of two-crop land, so as to make the rent-rate equal to the Collector's revenue calculation. Under such circumstances the landlord could only (in theory) have made a profit (1) on his own "home farm" lands, (2) on new cultivation, and (3) by miscellaneous levies and profits.

All lands were held either by tenants paying cash rents or by "Ādhiyār" men who cultivated on the terms of giving one-half the gross produce in kind. The latter

* If any proof were needed, the above would show conclusively that the Zamindar was *in origin* not the owner of the soil, but a (perhaps hereditary) ruler or official manager, taking the State dues, and not a contract-rent, from the cultivators.

system, Dr. Hamilton estimates, left them one-quarter the produce to live on. He was astonished that these "metayers" were very poorly off. There were also many landless farm laborers, who were the poorest of all. Small tenancies were the commonest, and above half of the tenants had one or two "ploughs" each.* On clay lands which bore one (rice) crop only in the year, they had only to work for six months, and for the rest of the year went elsewhere as day laborers, or in some other employ in sugar or indigo factories.

The poverty of the smaller tenants was attributed then, as now, to ignorance and improvidence. They never put by a farthing. The moment a man had a little surplus, he spent it in marriage feasts and the like. In consequence, they always had to borrow when the time came to pay rent or to buy seed-grain or plough cattle. They were given loans at heavy interest, or seed-rice in kind at a high price when the harvest was six months distant. They were then "forced to repay in kind just after the harvest, when the market was glutted by every necessitous person rushing to sell his produce at the same time." Very much the same thing happens at the present day, but in a less degree and in a diminishing number of cases. The whole system would have been intolerable, but that the larger farmers and managers were in fact obliged to show some consideration. If the cultivator became seriously discontented, as moving was no trouble to him, he would go off, and was sure to find waste or other land on a neighboring estate. "The village which he left is then for some years unoccupied, until the landlord can find a fugitive of the same kind; and, in general, he must use a good deal of solicitation before he can induce the (tenant) farmer with his dependants to settle." †

* He reckons five acres to "one plough." Three "ploughs" (fifteen acres) is now reckoned a fair but small holding.

† In early times the competition was not for land, but for tenants. At

I mentioned above that, in the case of tenants paying cash rents, the theory was that the rent in old established villages was no more than the government assessment rate. The real profit was there made, whether by a superior tenant or the landlord, in the form of high interest on the advances given in cash or kind, and in extra levies. As to these levies, the landlords generally courted the assistance of the larger farmers, so as to be able to allege their consent to a "cess" being charged all round. "A landlord or his agent assembles his people, and states that he is in want of money to build a house, to perform a pilgrimage, to celebrate some holiday, to marry a son or a daughter, or to alleviate the pecuniary distress in which he is involved, and solicits the assistance of his tenantry. The rich tenants have been previously gained, and give their consent to a general assessment, and the others follow their example rather than quarrel with people on whom they depend; but it is only the poor who pay." Thus, by conciliating a few larger tenants, the poor were kept drained of all the surplus that ought to enable them to buy their own stock and seed, without taking advances and getting into debt.

I cannot follow Dr. Hamilton in his estimate of the cost of cultivating and of the tenant farmer's living; but he shows clearly that the rent did not come to more than one-quarter of the gross produce, and that the farmers besides had the profit of their milk and their "plantation,"—fruit, bamboos, and so on. Still, the humbler classes were so preyed on by the heavy demands of interest on advances and by the exactions, not only of the landlord, as just described, but of his underlings of all sorts also, that they were in the poorest condition. "The general manner in which the agents spoke of the tenants

present conditions are reversed; but market rates of rent are in consequence better established, and the law of rent and rent-recovery has been much improved, first in 1859, and then in 1885.

convinced me that they considered them as subjects to whom they had a right to dictate law, and that this right was an excuse for whatever hardships they might choose to inflict." *

A great deal of what Dr. Hamilton noticed is true at the present day. Of course, prices are much higher. Laborers do not now receive 8 anas a month, besides food and clothing; and tenants have better legal security for a certain and actually reasonable rent. But no law can prevent the people from being preyed on by the landlord's agent and by his harpies of messengers and writers, if public spirit does not enable them to resist. The levy of extra charges and fines is rigidly prohibited by law, but no law can be operative if the people themselves do do not unite in refusing to pay such exactions. In the eastern districts, where there are no great landholders, the tenants have rather the upper hand. In the central districts, and especially northward in the Bihar districts, it is otherwise. The Tenant Law of 1885 did a great deal for the people; but the real (final) remedy is a proper survey and a record of all rights and interests in land by area, with reference to a cadastral map. This it is the interest of bad landlords to resist. It is, moreover, easy to stir up the ignorant tenants themselves in supposed opposition to it; for in former days "measurement" was always used *against* them, and they are easily taught by interested agitators to believe that it will be so now.

The landlord class has for many years enjoyed in Bengal a special privilege of contributing to the State less — by something like two-thirds — than landholders

* Dr. Hamilton believed that a very common way of injury was the widespread practice of giving receipts for less than was really paid. He thinks this and the practice of suing for more than is due is very bad. He remarks that such acts could (under the then existing law) be punished only with a money penalty. He is of opinion that it ought, when proved, to be punished with "transportation beyond the seas for some years, accompanied, of course, with loss of caste."

in other provinces contribute; and, although no one would deprive them of this guaranteed exemption, they must not be allowed to forget that in granting the privilege government expressly reserved the right to protect all classes and to enact laws for the purpose of securing the raiyats. That, of course, includes the levy of a rate to meet expenditure necessarily and directly incurred in effecting the protection. There is no reason in equity why the land-owners should not contribute fairly to the expenses of a survey by which they themselves will in the end benefit,—at least, all honest and well-intentioned proprietors will benefit; and those alone have any claim on our sympathies. In fact, if it were not for the general ignorance which prevails on the subject, and the persistent misrepresentations of a class who vaguely fear the burden of a temporary charge, and also, not improbably, fear that their own dealings will not bear the light, it would be regarded as incredible that a complicated system of tenancies and other interests should exist year after year, the population increasing, and subdivision of interests going on apace, and yet that no cadastral survey should have been made, and no map or record be available by aid of which any holding can be traced on the ground. Such a record, it is needless to say, exists in *all* other provinces under the British government in India.

B. H. BADEN-POWELL.